Ancient Egypt

First published in Great Britain in 1995
by Macdonald Young Books Ltd
Campus 400, Maylands Avenue, Hemel Hempstead, Herts HP2 7EZ

Conceived and produced by Weldon Owen Pty Limited
43 Victoria Street, McMahons Point, NSW 2060, Australia
A member of the Weldon Owen Group of Companies
Sydney • San Francisco • London
Copyright © 1995 Weldon Owen Pty Limited

Publisher: Sheena Coupe
Managing Editor: Rosemary McDonald
Project Editor: Ann B. Bingaman
Text Editor: Claire Craig
Educational Consultants: Richard L. Needham, Deborah A. Powell
Art Director: Sue Burk
Designer: Lyndel Donaldson
Series Design Consultants: Alex Arthur, Arthur Brown
Assistant Designer: Angela Pelizzari
Visual Research Coordinator: Jenny Mills
Visual Research: Amanda Weir
Production Director: Mick Bagnato
Production Coordinator: Simone Perryman
Vice-President International Sales: Stuart Laurence
Coeditions Director: Derek Barton

Text: Judith Simpson

Illustrators: Paul Bachem; Kerri Gibbs;
Mike Gorman; Christa Hook/Bernard Thornton Artists, UK;
Richard Hook/Bernard Thornton Artists, UK; Janet Jones; Iain McKellar;
Peter Mennim; Paul Newman; Darren Pattenden/Garden Studio;
Evert Ploeg; Trevor Ruth; Ray Sim; Mark Sofilas;
C. Winston Taylor; Steve Trevaskis; Rod Westblade

A catalogue record for this book is available from the British Library
ISBN 0-7500-1803-8.

Manufactured by Mandarin Offset
Printed in China

A Weldon Owen Production

Ancient Egypt

CONSULTING EDITOR

Dr George Hart
Staff Lecturer
The British Museum, London

MACDONALD YOUNG BOOKS

Contents

• AN ANCIENT WORLD •

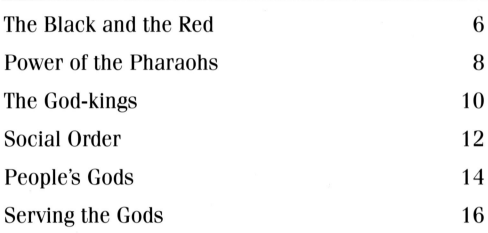

• THE WORLD BEYOND •

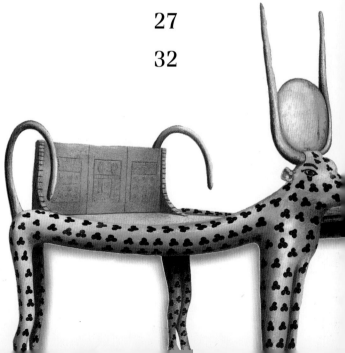

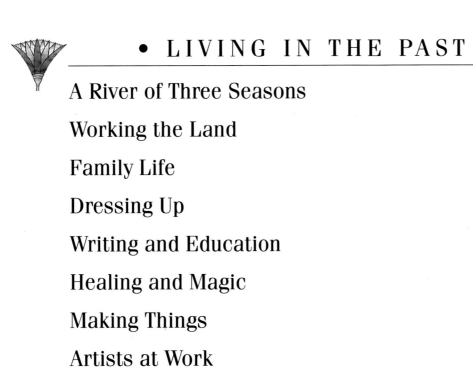

• LIVING IN THE PAST •

• FOREIGN AFFAIRS •

THE CLIFFS OF THEBES
Limestone cliffs line the western boundary of the valley at Thebes. Pharaohs built temples on the edge of the floodplain and tombs in the hills beyond.

Alexander's Alexandria
Alexander the Great invaded Egypt in 331 BC, and planned a great city called Alexandria.

MEDITERRANEAN SEA

Rosetta
Alexandria

LOWER EGYPT

Giza · Cairo
Memphis · Saqqara

Faiyum

SINAI DESERT

EASTERN DESERT

· Amarna

The monuments of Giza
The pyramids and the sphinx at Giza are landmarks of ancient Egypt, visible from a great distance across the desert.

WESTERN DESERT

LIBYA

UPPER EGYPT

Abydos ·

Queen Hatshepsut's temple
Queen Hatshepsut, who ruled as pharaoh, built a terraced temple at Deir el-Bahri on the west bank of the Nile. She filled the gardens with sweet-smelling plants.

Valley of the Kings

Karnak
· Luxor
Thebes

Edfu ·

Abu Simbel
Ramesses II ordered two huge temples to be built in the desert at Abu Simbel in Nubia. They were carved out of the sandstone cliffs.

· Abu Simbel

Temples at Karnak
Karnak was an important religious centre. Stone columns with elaborately carved tops supported the heavy roofs of the huge temples.

NUBIA

CUSH

NUBIAN DESERT

· AN ANCIENT WORLD ·

The Black and the Red

People began to live beside the River Nile many thousands of years ago. The river cut through the desert and provided them with water. The valley of Upper Egypt in the south formed a long narrow strip; the delta of Lower Egypt in the north spread out across the river mouth. Every year, floods washed thick mud over the banks and left good soil behind. Early Egyptians called this the "Black Land" and used it for growing crops. Beyond it was the "Red Land", an immense stony waste where it hardly ever rained and nothing useful grew. Where the Black Land ended, the Red Land began. A person could stand with one foot on fertile ground and the other on dry sand. Wolves and jackals hunted along the edges of the desert, but human enemies were seldom able to cross it and attack ancient Egypt.

6

MARSH HUNT
The hunter felled birds with his throwing stick after his trained cat had startled them from the papyrus reeds.

RED SEA

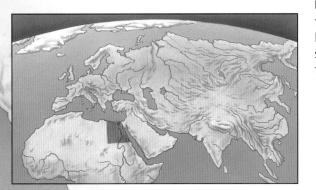

LAND OF THE LOTUS
People in modern times have likened ancient Egypt to a lotus plant, with its valley as the stem and its delta as the flower.

THE CIVILISATION OF ANCIENT EGYPT

Hippopotamus hunt

New stone-age pottery

LAND OF TWO KINGDOMS
Begins about 3000 BC.
Ditches were dug to irrigate the land and villages became more established. In 3100 BC, Narmer united Upper and Lower Egypt.

Narmer's palette shows his victory

Tuthmosis IV

OLD STONE AGE
Before 12,000 BC.
The earliest Egyptians hunted lions, goats and wild cattle on land, and hippopotamuses and crocodiles in the river marshes.

NEW STONE AGE
Begins about 4500 BC.
During this period, people discovered fire for cooking. They learnt to herd animals and to grow grain.

RULE OF THE PHARAOHS
2920 BC to 332 BC.
Egypt was strong for much of this time. Monuments were built and trade with foreign countries developed.

Discover more in A River of Three Seasons

Power of the Pharaohs

The civilisation we call ancient Egypt started about 5,000 years ago, when the rule of the pharaohs began. They made Egypt a rich and powerful nation, admired throughout the ancient world. They also ordered the building of great temples for their gods and elaborate tombs for themselves. Some pharaohs, such as Pepy II, came to the throne when they were very young and stayed in power for many years. Sons inherited their father's throne. Pharaohs' wives were also important, but few women ever ruled the country. Teams of workers crafted beautiful objects for the pharaohs and their families. They used materials such as semi-precious stones and gold from the desert mines. The royal couple often displayed their riches in public. Processions, receptions for foreign visitors and visits to the temples were opportunities to show the power of the pharaohs.

A ROYAL JOURNEY
The magnificent royal barge gliding down the river reminded people of the wealth and importance of their god-king and his "Great Royal Wife".

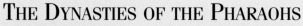

THE DYNASTIES OF THE PHARAOHS

ARCHAIC PERIOD
2920 BC to 2575 BC.
Upper and Lower Egypt were united. Building programs included impressive monuments in Saqqara and Abydos.

Stone vase

OLD KINGDOM
2575 BC to 2134 BC.
This period was also known as the Age of Pyramids. Crafts and architecture developed. Picture symbols, called hieroglyphs, were used to write the texts inside the pyramids.

Female brewer

FIRST INTERMEDIATE PERIOD
2134 BC to 2040 BC.
At the end of the sixth dynasty, a series of weak pharaohs ruled. Local officials called nomarchs struggled for more power. Low Nile floods caused widespread famine.

MIDDLE KINGDOM
2040 BC to 1640 BC.
Strong pharaohs united the country again and trade revived. The twelfth-dynasty pharaohs organised canals and reservoirs for better irrigation.

King Mentuhotpe II

Q: When did the strongest pharaohs rule?

PEOPLE IN WAITING
Officials and tribute bearers, soldiers and slaves stood by the immense columns of the temple to receive their pharaoh.

FIT FOR A PHARAOH
A sphinx guarded the prow. The rest of the barge was covered with gold and inlaid with semi-precious stones.

SAFE LANDING
Oarsmen were skilled at bringing the boat smoothly to rest beside the quay.

SECOND INTERMEDIATE PERIOD
1640 BC to 1550 BC.
The pharaohs lost control. The Hyksos from the Near East settled in the delta region.

NEW KINGDOM
1550 BC to 1070 BC.
Ahmose ousted the Hyksos. The pharaohs who followed him expanded Egypt's frontiers to form an empire.

Chariot

THIRD INTERMEDIATE PERIOD
1070 BC to 712 BC.
Power was divided between the pharaohs and the high priests.

LATE PERIOD
712 BC to 332 BC.
The Egyptian conquerors became the conquered. Successive invasions of Nubians, Assyrians and Persians took over Egypt. In 332 BC, Alexander the Great freed Egypt from Persian rule.

Alexander the Great

Discover more in Defending the Kingdom

9

The God-kings

An ancient Egyptian creation myth tells how the god Osiris was sent by Re, the sun-god, to rule the country. The Egyptians believed that all pharaohs were god-kings. The god-kings took part in many ceremonies. They had to dress, eat and even wash in a special way, and every day they went to the temple to offer food to their ancestors. People expected pharaohs to be physically strong, expert at hunting and able to lead the army to victory in battle. Their subjects thought the god-kings controlled the flowing and flooding of the Nile and the growth of crops, as well as the country's success in foreign trade. Everyone knelt and kissed the ground when they approached the royal person. The pharaohs continued to be worshipped even after they had died and joined the god Osiris in the kingdom of the dead.

DID YOU KNOW?

When Queen Hatshepsut's husband died, she took over government and ruled for her stepson Tuthmosis III, who was only five. She held power for about 20 years. Statues show her wearing the false beard of kingship.

MARK OF A PHARAOH
Oval shapes containing hieroglyphs were called cartouches. Two of them make up a pharaoh's name. Cartouches have helped Egyptologists decipher the ancient Egyptian language.

Haremhab

THE GREAT ROYAL WIFE

Pharaohs' wives were also regarded as gods, and shared their husbands' wealth. This painted limestone bust of Queen Nefertiti shows her wearing a crown and necklace rich with jewels. Nefertiti was the wife of Akhenaten. She helped him establish a new city at Amarna on the east bank of the River Nile in Middle Egypt. Women rarely ruled the country unless it was for a short time at the end of the dynasty when there were no men to take over. Hatshepsut was the only strong woman ruler.

COURT VISITORS
Foreigners, such as this group from the Middle East, often appeared at the pharaoh's court. They came to offer gifts or to discuss trade agreements.

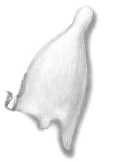

White crown

Red crown

CHOICE OF CROWNS
Pharaohs might wear the white crown of Upper Egypt, the red crown of Lower Egypt, the double crown of a united Egypt, the atef crown of Osiris or the blue crown.

Double crown

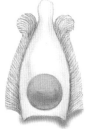

Atef crown

Blue crown

COMFORT AT COURT
Slaves fanned the pharaoh and his wife on their comfortable cushioned thrones. The king held a crook and flail—symbols of power linking him to the god Osiris. He also wore a crown and a false beard.

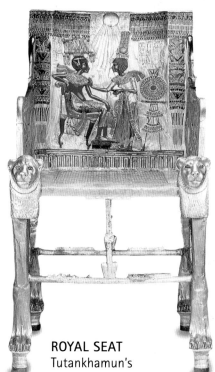

ROYAL SEAT
Tutankhamun's wooden throne, covered in gold leaf, pictured the young king with his wife Ankhsenamon.

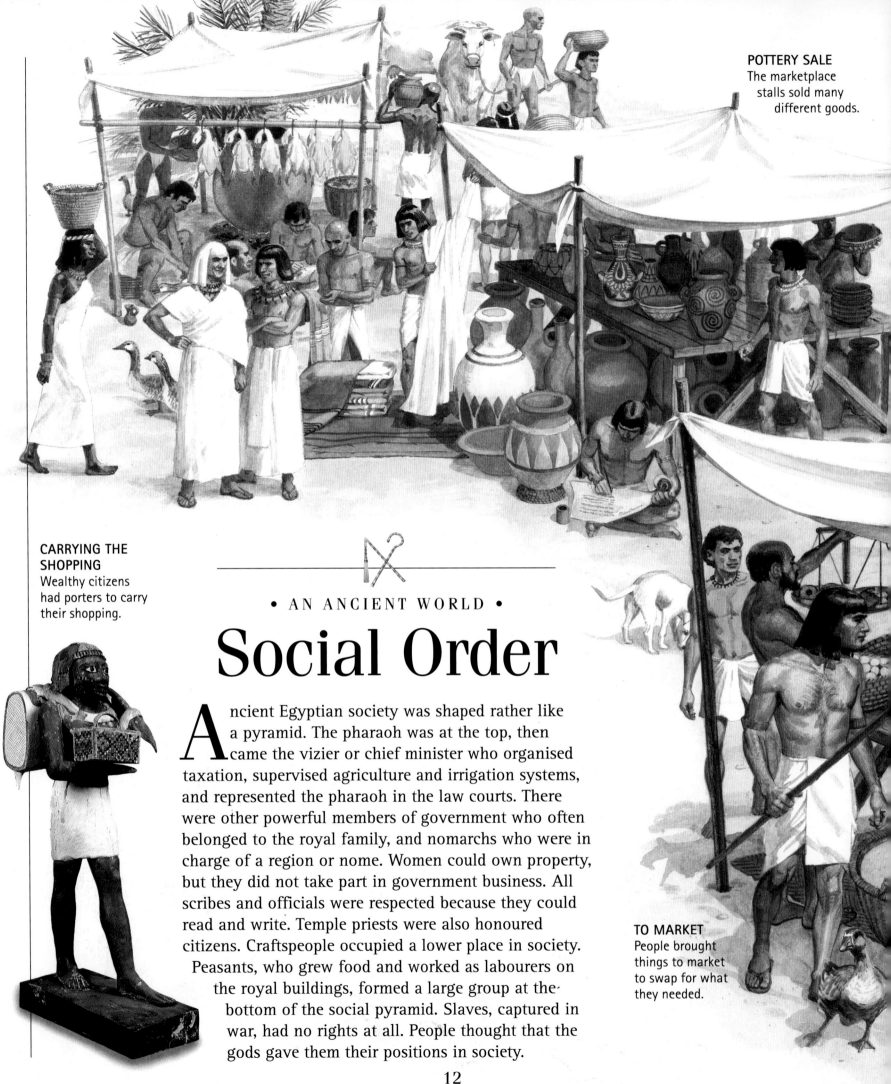

CARRYING THE SHOPPING
Wealthy citizens had porters to carry their shopping.

• AN ANCIENT WORLD •

Social Order

Ancient Egyptian society was shaped rather like a pyramid. The pharaoh was at the top, then came the vizier or chief minister who organised taxation, supervised agriculture and irrigation systems, and represented the pharaoh in the law courts. There were other powerful members of government who often belonged to the royal family, and nomarchs who were in charge of a region or nome. Women could own property, but they did not take part in government business. All scribes and officials were respected because they could read and write. Temple priests were also honoured citizens. Craftspeople occupied a lower place in society. Peasants, who grew food and worked as labourers on the royal buildings, formed a large group at the bottom of the social pyramid. Slaves, captured in war, had no rights at all. People thought that the gods gave them their positions in society.

TO MARKET
People brought things to market to swap for what they needed.

COUNTING THE CATTLE

An ancient Egyptian's wealth was measured in cattle rather than in coins. Meketre, who was once mayor of Thebes, had a healthy herd of animals. This model from his tomb shows them being counted in front of their master and other officials. This was a yearly event of great importance. Government scribes came to record the numbers carefully on papyrus. Later, they would calculate how many beasts Meketre must give the pharaoh as a tax payment.

WOMEN'S WORK
Some tasks such as grinding grain, baking and harvesting, spinning and weaving flax, were done more often by women than by men.

FRESH FOOD
In Egypt's hot climate, people had to shop daily for fresh provisions. Few foods were dried for storage.

WEIGHING THE GOODS
Ancient Egyptians did not use money. Stallholders weighed produce in copper weights, called debens, and priced goods accordingly. A goat worth 1 deben could be exchanged for vegetables weighing 1 deben.

HOME HELP
Bes had the ears, mane and tail of a lion. He brought happiness to the home and protected it from evil.

THOTH'S OTHER DISGUISE
Thoth, god of writing and knowledge, was sometimes shown as a baboon. At other times he was represented by a man with an ibis's head.

People's Gods

Religion was a very important part of the lives of ancient Egyptians. They worshipped hundreds of gods. Some, such as the sun-god Re or Amun-Re, were honoured by everyone throughout the land in a festival that lasted for a month in the flood season when farmers did no work in the fields. In addition, each of the 42 regions (nomes) adopted a different god to look after its affairs. At home, people turned to lesser gods for help with everyday problems. Many gods were depicted as animals—for example, Bastet the cat, goddess of love and joy—or as human figures with the heads of animals and birds, such as ibis-headed Thoth, god of knowledge. The gods had families too. Osiris and Isis were husband and wife with a son called Horus.

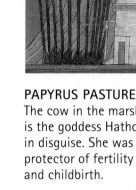

PAPYRUS PASTURE
The cow in the marsh is the goddess Hathor in disguise. She was a protector of fertility and childbirth.

LIONESS-HEADED
The goddess Sakhmet the Powerful was shown with a woman's body and the head of a lioness.

Hathor

Re

Thoth

A PARADE OF GODS
Seven of the most important gods are depicted here. Six of them carry the sacred ankh, which symbolised life.

GOD OF THE UNDERWORLD
Osiris was shown with a crown of reeds and ostrich feathers. He carried a crook and flail to show that he was king of the underworld.

FEEDING THE BABY
Isis cared for Horus and hid him from his wicked uncle Seth, until he grew up. Seth murdered Osiris and tried to kill Horus too. Isis helped Horus to get revenge for his father's death by using her magic to trick Seth.

Anubis

Osiris

Isis

Horus

JACKAL GOD
The god Anubis was sometimes represented as a jackal and sometimes as a man with a jackal's head. He looked after the place of mummification and supervised the priests' embalming work.

THE SUN-GOD'S DAILY JOURNEY
The ancient Egyptians travelled mainly by river boat. They believed that every 24 hours, the great sun-god Amun-Re made a voyage across the sky as though he were on the waters of the Nile. At night, he sailed through the underworld of the spirits and emerged from this dark place at sunrise each day.

Discover more in Journey to Osiris

15

Serving the Gods

FLAG BEARER
Horus, the falcon-god, sits on top of a pole that once held a flag in a temple procession.

Ancient Egyptians believed that the spirits of the gods dwelt within the temples. Many people were employed to look after these enormous buildings, which were the focus of every community. An inner sanctuary in the heart of each temple protected the statue of the god. Only the pharaoh and the high priest were allowed to enter this sacred place. The people could leave written prayers outside the temples, but they never saw the statues of the gods. Even in processions, portable shrines hid the figures from public view. Women played some part in temple ritual but the high priests were men. They washed, dressed and applied make-up to the statues as though they were alive. The priests lived by strict rules of cleanliness. They bathed four times a day, shaved their heads and bodies, and wore fine, white linen gowns.

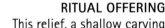
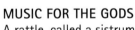

PROVISIONS FOR A GOD
The high priest or the pharaoh carried food and drink to the sanctuary three times a day. Before each meal, they washed the statue and clothed it in fresh linen.

MUSIC FOR THE GODS
A rattle, called a sistrum, was used in temple rituals. It was the symbol of the goddess Hathor.

RITUAL OFFERING
This relief, a shallow carving in stone, shows Ramesses II offering incense to Horus.

ENTERTAINING THE GODS
In the temple courtyards, women sang, danced, and put on acrobatic displays for the gods.

ON FESTIVAL DAYS
The priests placed the god's statue in a shrine and carried it in procession round the outside of the temple.

SEALING THE SANCTUARY
When the high priest left the shrine, he sealed the doors with a mud seal.

TEMPLE FOR THE SUN-GOD
Treasure from successful military expeditions helped pay for the temple of Amun-Re at Karnak. Central columns, higher than a nine-storey building, are crowned with carved papyrus heads. The walls are inscribed with records of Sethos I's battle victories. The grounds once included gardens, orchards and living quarters for temple workers.

Amun-Re

FIRST SERVANT OF THE GOD
The high priests represented the pharaoh. They also supervised other priests who attended to the daily routines of the temple.

Discover more in The Valley of the Kings

STRANGE BUT TRUE

In the sixteenth century, ground-up mummies were used in European medicines. One French king took a mixture of mummy and powdered rhubarb to cure his battle wounds. It made him violently ill.

THE WINGS OF ISIS
One corner of Ramesses III's stone sarcophagus is carved with the protective figure of Isis with outstretched wings.

TUTANKHAMUN'S MASK
This life-size mask, engraved with magic spells, protected the head of Tutankhamun's mummy. The mask is made from gold inlaid with semi-precious stones.

• THE WORLD BEYOND •

Preparing for the Afterlife

The ancient Egyptians enjoyed life and wanted all their earthly pleasures in the afterlife. They believed that every person had vital spiritual parts. The *Ka* was the life force, created at birth and released by death; the *Ba* was like the soul. In order to live forever, the *Ka* and *Ba* had to be united with the body after death and so it was important to preserve the corpse. Poor people were buried in the desert where the sand dried their bodies. Food, tools and jewellery were laid beside them for use in the kingdom of Osiris. The wealthy could afford to have their bodies mummified and placed with their possessions in special tombs. The coffins were enclosed in large stone boxes, which were later called sarcophagi, to protect them from tomb robbers or attacks from hungry wild animals.

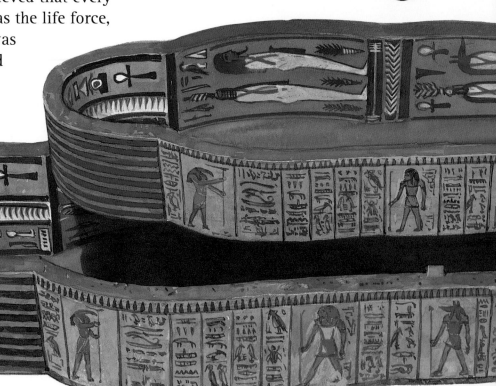

18

Lid of outer mummy case

Lid of inner mummy case

Wrapped mummy with mask

Bottom of inner mummy case

TUTANKHAMUN'S MUMMY
The king's body was carefully taken from its wrappings and then photographed. Scientists have not been able to find out what killed the young pharaoh.

BA BIRD
This picture of the hovering *Ba* bird is from the scribe Ani's *Book of the Dead*. It shows the spell that will return Ani's important *Ba* to his mummified body.

MUMMY CASES
Coffins made of wood or cartonnage, a kind of papier-mâché, were painted with pictures of gods, spells and many hieroglyphs praising the owner. The inner coffin fitted inside one or two outer cases.

Bottom of outer mummy case

MUMMIES AND MODERN SCIENCE

Modern technology allows scientists to examine mummies without opening the coffins or damaging the bodies. At St Thomas's Hospital in London, England, the body of Tjentmutengebtiu, a 20-year-old woman, was analysed with the help of an advanced X-ray process called CAT scanning.

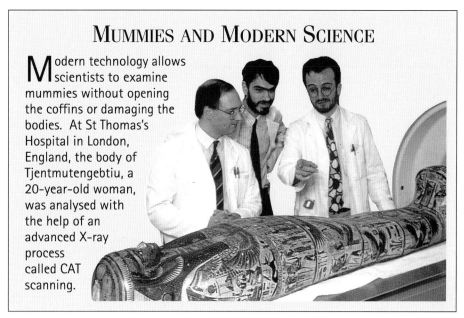

Discover more in Artists at Work

19

Mummies in the Making

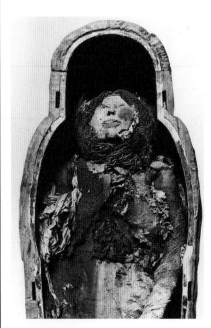

Mummification is the process of slowly drying a dead body to stop it rotting. In ancient Egypt, the process took about 70 days. Embalming priests removed the liver, lungs, stomach and intestines and stored them in four special little coffins called canopic jars. Later, these were placed in the tomb beside the mummy. The priests also removed the brain, but left the heart to be weighed by the god Anubis. They washed the corpse in palm wine and covered it with a natural salt called natron to absorb the moisture. After 40 days, embalmers rubbed the skin with oils, packed the body with spices, linen, sawdust and sand to reshape it, and wrapped it in layer upon layer of linen bandages that had been soaked in resin. They placed magic spells and good luck charms between the strips. Finally, they sealed the mummy in its case.

EYES OF GOLD
In the last years of ancient Egypt lifelike representations of eyes made from gold leaf were placed over the eye-sockets of corpses.

AIR PURIFIER
The priests burned incense to sweeten the air while they prepared the mummy, working as quickly as possible.

EMBALMING WORKSHOPS
Teams of embalming priests mummified bodies in workshops where all the special tools and equipment were kept.

CANOPIC JARS
The Sons of Horus protected different organs: Imset for the liver, Ha'py for the lungs, Duamutef for the stomach, Qebehsenuf for the intestines.

A BAD JOB
Not all embalmers were good at their job. This queen's puffed and cracked face was the result of overstuffing.

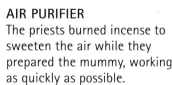

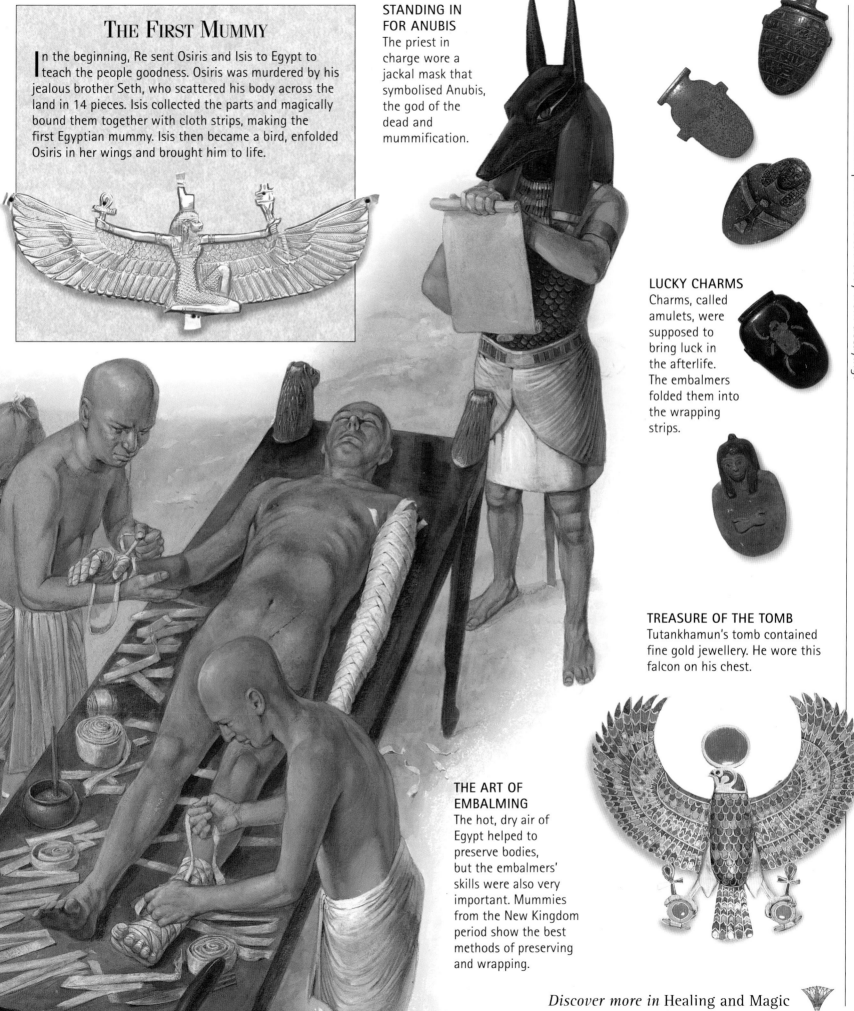

THE FIRST MUMMY

In the beginning, Re sent Osiris and Isis to Egypt to teach the people goodness. Osiris was murdered by his jealous brother Seth, who scattered his body across the land in 14 pieces. Isis collected the parts and magically bound them together with cloth strips, making the first Egyptian mummy. Isis then became a bird, enfolded Osiris in her wings and brought him to life.

STANDING IN FOR ANUBIS
The priest in charge wore a jackal mask that symbolised Anubis, the god of the dead and mummification.

LUCKY CHARMS
Charms, called amulets, were supposed to bring luck in the afterlife. The embalmers folded them into the wrapping strips.

TREASURE OF THE TOMB
Tutankhamun's tomb contained fine gold jewellery. He wore this falcon on his chest.

THE ART OF EMBALMING
The hot, dry air of Egypt helped to preserve bodies, but the embalmers' skills were also very important. Mummies from the New Kingdom period show the best methods of preserving and wrapping.

Discover more in Healing and Magic

21

Journey to Osiris

The "Opening of the Mouth" was one of the most important funeral ceremonies in the final preparation of the mummy. The deceased's family recited spells while priests sprinkled water and used special instruments to touch the mummy on the lips. Without this ritual, the dead person would not be able to eat, drink or move about in the afterlife. Before anyone could qualify for eternal life, the stern judge Anubis weighed their heart against the feather of truth to see how well they had behaved on Earth. Anubis threw the unworthy hearts to the monster Ammit, "Devourer of the Dead", and the owners went no further. Those who passed the test continued on the dangerous and difficult journey to the kingdom of Osiris. Magic symbols painted on the mummy's case were designed to protect the traveller along the way.

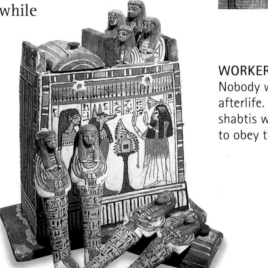

WORKERS FOR ETERNITY
Nobody wanted to work in the afterlife. Model servants called shabtis were placed in the tombs to obey the god Osiris's commands.

Hunefer   Anubis   Anubis   Ammit, Devourer of the Dead   Thoth

ESSENTIALS FOR THE AFTERLIFE

We know much about the lives of ancient Egyptians from the contents of their tombs. Tutankhamun's tomb contained his childhood toys, 116 baskets of fruit, 40 jars of wine, and boxes of roast duck, bread and cake. Musicians were buried with their instruments and women with their beauty kits. Eye make-up was included for everyone. Model boats provided transport to the kingdom of Osiris.

STRANGE BUT TRUE

Thousands of mummified cats were found in many tombs. In the nineteenth century, about 300,000 cat mummies were shipped to England where they were ground up into garden fertiliser.

WEIGHING THE HEART

This is the mummy's most testing moment. Ammit sits beneath the scales, hungry for sinful hearts. The scribe god, Thoth, takes notes. If all goes well, Osiris will welcome the newcomer, Hunefer.

MUMMIFIED MENAGERIE

People thought that animals were messengers of the gods and many were mummified, including calves, crocodiles and cats.

Hunefer   Horus   Osiris

23

Set in Stone

Many ancient Egyptian stone monuments still stand in the desert today. Although moisture, wind, sandstorms and tourists have damaged them, the pyramids, tombs, temples and colossal statues tell us much about the ideas, beliefs and technology of the people who built them. These incredibly complicated projects required expert skills and a huge workforce. Astronomers studied the stars to determine the best sites, mathematicians and architects calculated the measurements, stonemasons shaped the blocks, and overseers organised the teams of several thousand labourers. Craftsmen worked soft stones with bronze and copper chisels. They pounded harder rocks with balls of dolerite, then rubbed the surface smooth with quartz sand. The Great Pyramids at Giza were faced originally with gleaming white Tura limestone and may have been capped with gold.

SHIPPING THE STONE
Carpenters built cargo vessels at the Nile shipyards to carry stone blocks from the quarries to the building sites.

THE PYRAMIDS OF GIZA
Khufu's Great Pyramid, the biggest of three massive pyramids at Giza, is the largest stone building in the world. It is 146 m (479 ft) high and contains nearly two-and-a-half million blocks of limestone.

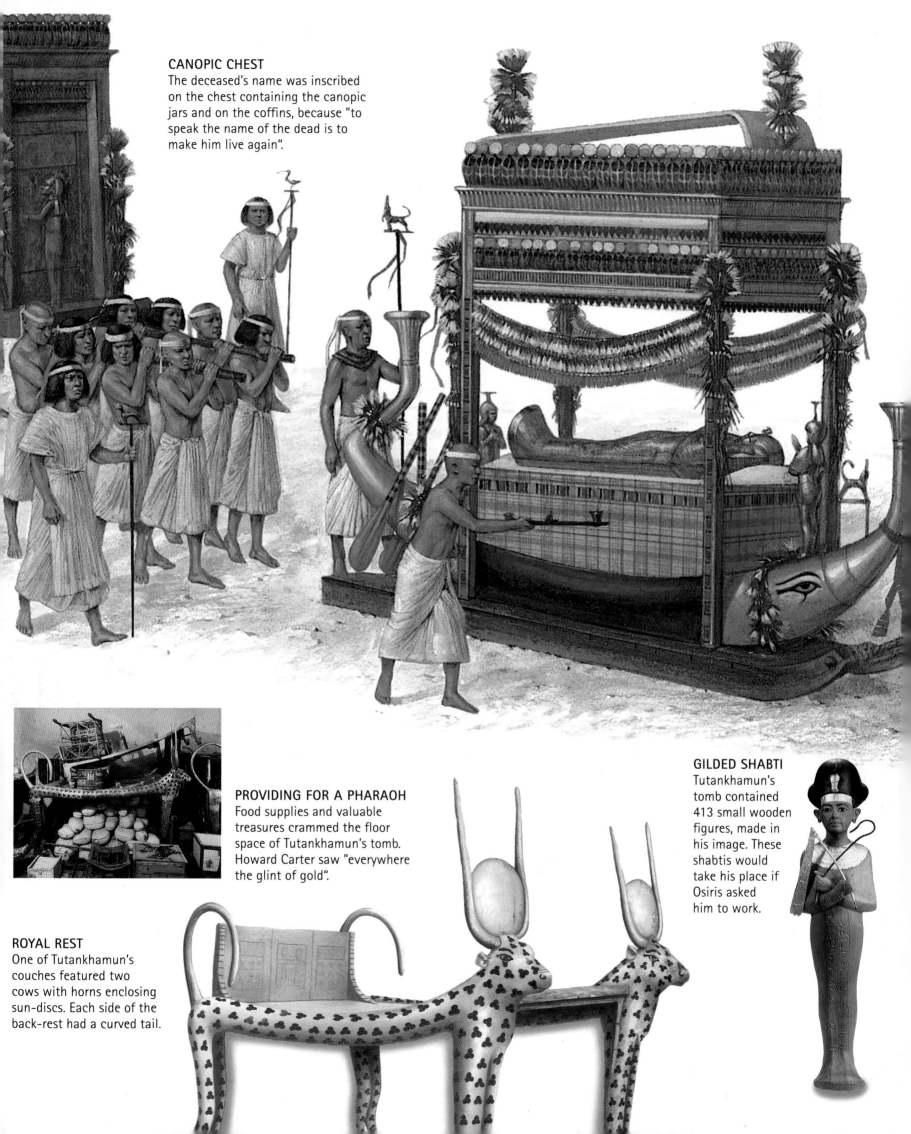

CANOPIC CHEST
The deceased's name was inscribed on the chest containing the canopic jars and on the coffins, because "to speak the name of the dead is to make him live again".

PROVIDING FOR A PHARAOH
Food supplies and valuable treasures crammed the floor space of Tutankhamun's tomb. Howard Carter saw "everywhere the glint of gold".

GILDED SHABTI
Tutankhamun's tomb contained 413 small wooden figures, made in his image. These shabtis would take his place if Osiris asked him to work.

ROYAL REST
One of Tutankhamun's couches featured two cows with horns enclosing sun-discs. Each side of the back-rest had a curved tail.

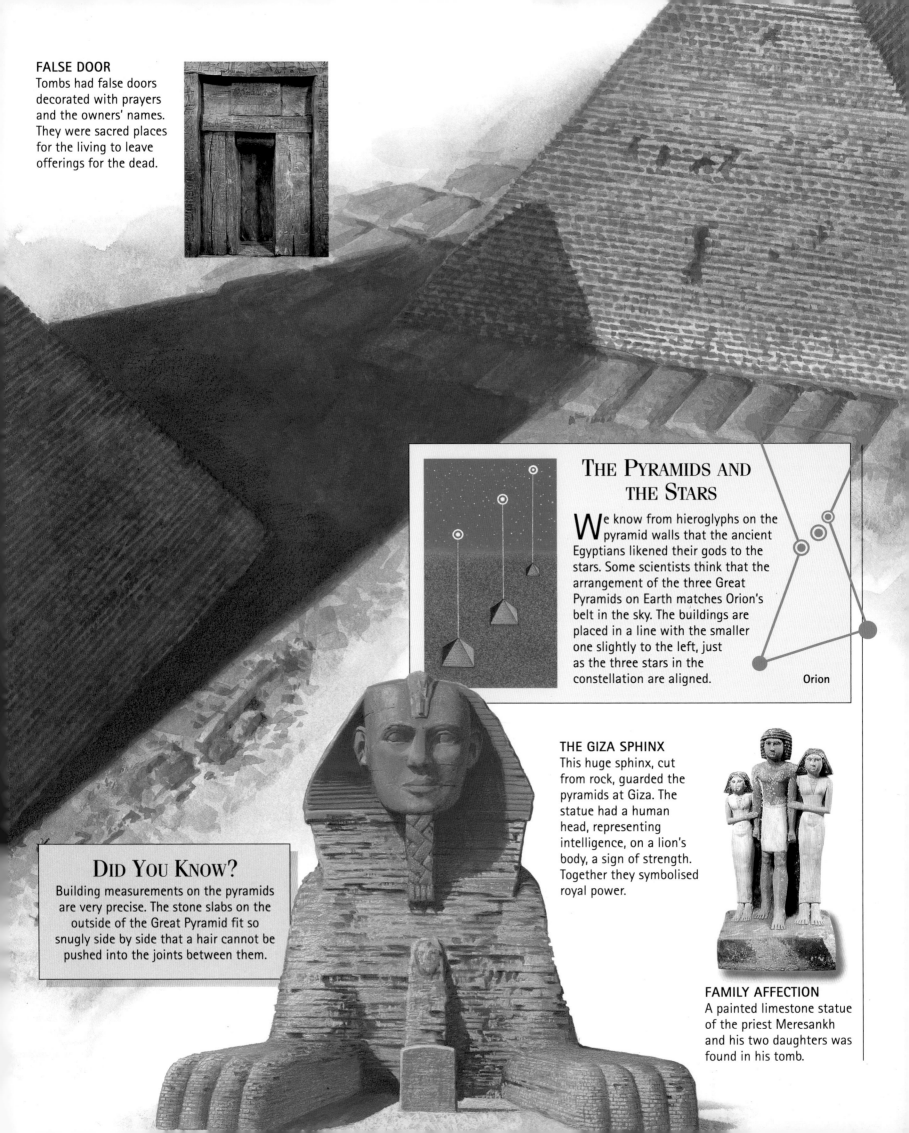

FALSE DOOR
Tombs had false doors decorated with prayers and the owners' names. They were sacred places for the living to leave offerings for the dead.

THE PYRAMIDS AND THE STARS
We know from hieroglyphs on the pyramid walls that the ancient Egyptians likened their gods to the stars. Some scientists think that the arrangement of the three Great Pyramids on Earth matches Orion's belt in the sky. The buildings are placed in a line with the smaller one slightly to the left, just as the three stars in the constellation are aligned.

Orion

THE GIZA SPHINX
This huge sphinx, cut from rock, guarded the pyramids at Giza. The statue had a human head, representing intelligence, on a lion's body, a sign of strength. Together they symbolised royal power.

DID YOU KNOW?
Building measurements on the pyramids are very precise. The stone slabs on the outside of the Great Pyramid fit so snugly side by side that a hair cannot be pushed into the joints between them.

FAMILY AFFECTION
A painted limestone statue of the priest Meresankh and his two daughters was found in his tomb.

Building a Pyramid

Step pyramid

Bent pyramid

True pyramid

BUILDING A PYRAMID
The pyramid's base was square; the four sides almost identical in length. The workers built the core first, then they dragged the facing blocks up ramps, working from the top downwards.

The Old Kingdom was the Age of Pyramids. The mummified bodies of pharaohs were laid to rest in these mansions of eternity. Each enormous tomb had a burial chamber deep inside. The surrounding spaces were filled with objects for the king's eternal comfort. The first pyramids were a series of stepped platforms. The pharaoh was supposed to climb this giant stairway to the sun. Later pyramids had smooth sloping sides to form a ramp so the pharaoh could go up to the sky on it. Building these great structures involved a great deal of time and was hazardous work. It probably took more than 20 years to complete Pharaoh Khufu's Great Pyramid. Many men crushed and broke bones, or slipped and fell to their death. Labourers believed that helping to construct a pyramid gave them a share in the king's afterlife.

CHANGING SHAPE
The architect Imhotep designed the first step pyramid at Saqqara for Pharaoh Djoser. The bent pyramid was a stage in the development of the true pyramid.

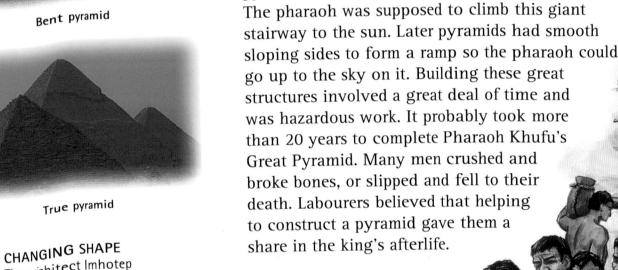

ROLLING THE ROCK
Each block weighed about the same as a male hippopotamus. Labourers used smooth wooden rollers coated with fine mud to help them haul the stones across the desert.

FURNISHING THE TOMB
Servants carried food and other things to place in the tomb. They believed that worldly goods were used in the afterlife.

ROYAL FANFARE
Silver trumpets with painted wooden cores were found in Tutankhamun's tomb.

ON GUARD
Two life-sized, varnished, wooden statues of Tutankhamun, dressed in gold leaf, guarded his burial chamber.

• THE WORLD BEYOND •

The Valley of the Kings

Far from the floodplain of the Nile, the Valley of the Kings lies deep in the western desert cliffs near Thebes. After the Age of Pyramids, pharaohs and wealthy people had their tombs built here. They hoped the isolated valley would protect them from grave robbers and they built separate temples to mislead thieves. Some of the tombs had concealed entrances cut high into the rocks. Corridor walls within the tombs had scenes and texts describing the journey to the afterlife. These deep passages led to the "Hall of Gold"—the mummy's final resting-place. All but one of the burial chambers we know about were plundered before the end of the ancient Egyptian civilisation. Only Tutankhamun lay undisturbed until 1922, when Lord Carnarvon and an English Egyptologist, Howard Carter, discovered this pharaoh's golden treasures.

1 King's chamber
2 Queen's chamber
3 Underground chamber
4 Grand gallery
5 Entrance

INSIDE
This diagram shows the layout of rooms and passageways inside the Great Pyramid. The king's chamber is at the heart.

LAST VOYAGE TO ETERNITY

In 1954, Egyptian archaeologists found a wooden barge sealed in a pit next to the Great Pyramid. The barge had been pulled apart to fit into the chamber. Markings showed that it had been in water at some time. It probably carried Khufu's body along the Nile to its resting place.

STRANGE BUT TRUE

When the boat pit at the Great Pyramid was opened, hot air rushed out. Egyptian archaeologist Kamal el Mallakh said, "I smelt incense ... I smelt time ... I smelt centuries ... I smelt history itself".

Discover more in Power of the Pharaohs

QUEEN NEFERTARI
Nefertari was the favourite wife of Ramesses II. She was buried in the Valley of the Queens at Deir el-Medina, West Thebes. Ramesses had "possessor of charm, sweetness and love" inscribed on her tomb.

OPENING THE MOUTH
This scene is painted on the wall of the tomb of Inherkha at Deir el-Medina. Here a priest is offering holy water to the mummy—a part of the Opening of the Mouth ceremony.

Burial chamber

Antechamber

Treasury

Annexe

Corridor

TUTANKHAMUN'S TOMB
Tutankhamun's tomb is the smallest royal tomb in the Valley of the Kings. The antechamber contained large beds and chariots. The annexe and the treasury were full of smaller, more precious objects.

WEEPING WOMEN
Hired mourners led the procession. These women were paid to wail loudly and cover their heads with dust. Behind them walked officials, and then came the family group.

CAREFUL CARTER
Howard Carter patiently chipped away hardened black oils from Tutankhamun's third and innermost coffin. It was made of solid gold.

DEIR EL-MEDINA
The tombs in the Valley of the Kings were made by royal workers who lived at Deir el-Medina. This village existed for the 500 years or so that the pharaohs were buried in their desert retreat. Scribal records tell us that the well-organised workforce was paid with government provisions and had one day off in ten. Craftspeople often had highly decorated tombs of their own and were buried with attractive grave goods, such as this painted terracotta jar.

FUNERAL PROCESSION
The funeral procession travelled slowly towards the tomb. Mourners dragged the mummy overland by sledge and crossed the river by barge.

RITUAL CEREMONIES
Priests walked beside the coffin burning incense and sprinkling water to purify the path. Butchers slaughtered cattle at the tomb.

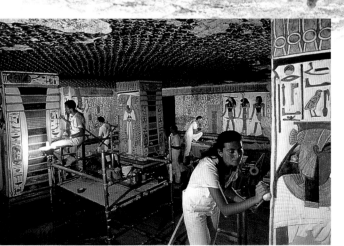

MENDING THE MURALS
In 1986, Italian artists began restoring the flaking paint on the walls of Queen Nefertari's tomb. This work took six years.

STRANGE BUT TRUE
The ancient Egyptians believed the goddess Meretseger guarded the Valley of the Kings. She was represented as a cobra and her venom was supposed to blind or poison grave robbers and so protect the tombs.

THE TEMPLE OF HATSHEPSUT

Hatshepsut ordered her great temple to be built on the west bank of the Nile. Sloping ramps connected terraces that jutted out from the rocky backdrop on three levels. By the end of the nineteenth century, little remained except a pile of rubble and sand.

COLOURED COLUMNS
The temple of the goddess Isis stands on the island of Philae. When this lithograph was made in 1846, some colour still remained on the columns in the hall.

• THE WORLD BEYOND •

Great Temples

Many pharaohs ordered temples to be constructed for themselves as well as for the gods. Some of the temples were attached to pharaohs' tombs, erected in separate places or added to other buildings such as the one at Karnak. Temple complexes included vast statues, soaring columns, school rooms, storehouses and workshops, and spacious gardens. By the time Ramesses II came to power in 1290 BC, many magnificent monuments had already been built throughout ancient Egypt. He added several others during his reign of more than 60 years. The most impressive one was at Abu Simbel in the Nubian desert. The labourers chipped away the side of a hill to make the south front and then hollowed out a huge space behind it for the interior. Hatshepsut, Amenophis III, Sethos I and Ramesses III were also great temple builders.

ON A GRAND SCALE
Massive granite statues of Ramesses II stood inside and outside his temple at Abu Simbel. A single foot was taller than an adult. Shallow reliefs, carved on the north and south walls, record Ramesses II's battle victories.

THE COLOSSI OF MEMNON
Two colossal stone statues are all that remain of Amenophis III's monument on the Nile's west bank.

DID YOU KNOW?

Twice a year, the shadowy interior of Ramesses II's temple is pierced by the rays of the rising sun, which illuminate the four statues in the temple's sanctuary.

RESCUING ABU SIMBEL

When the Aswan Dam was built across the River Nile in the 1960s, it created Lake Nasser. Many of the Nubian temples were moved to prevent them from being flooded.

A River of Three Seasons

TRAVELLING SOUTH
The hieroglyph "to travel south" was a boat in full sail catching the northerly wind to help propel the craft upstream.

TRAVELLING NORTH
River transport and walking were the main means of travelling. The hieroglyph "to travel north" was a boat with the sail down.

When the Greek traveller Herodotus saw ancient Egypt he called it "the gift of the Nile" and nobody has ever described it better. The river was a highway for transport and trade. It provided fish and larger game in the form of hippopotamuses and crocodiles. It sustained marshes where papyrus reeds and lotus plants grew and where waterfowl could be caught for food. It supplied water for drinking and washing. Every year, almost without fail, floodwaters from the lakes and mountain springs of eastern Africa, which fed the Nile's tributaries, washed down fertile silt. The river divided the farmers' calendar into three seasons. The flood time, the "time of inundation" when all work stopped, lasted from July to October. The "time of emergence", allotted to ploughing and sowing, ran from November to February. Finally, the "time of harvest" occupied March to June.

DID YOU KNOW?
It was more usual for men to wash dirty laundry in the river. Women were excused from these duties because of the constant threat from dangerous crocodiles along the river banks.

FISHING ON THE NILE
Fish from the river could be harpooned, caught with hooks and lines, or swept up in nets made from papyrus twine. They were part of the diet of ancient Egyptians.

PAPYRUS FOR MANY PURPOSES

Many years ago, papyrus grew plentifully along the banks of the Nile and in the delta swamps. The ancient Egyptians used it to make excellent paper. Some river boats were crafted from bundles of papyrus stalks; others were rigged with strong ropes made from its twisted fibres. This reed could also be woven into boxes, baskets, mats, sieves and sandals.

HUNTING GEESE
This scene from a tomb shows the sport of wealthy Egyptians—hunting with throwsticks.

SPEAR FISHING
This statuette shows Tutankhamun about to hurl his spear, probably into a hippopotamus. In his left hand he holds a cord for binding his prey.

• LIVING IN THE PAST •

Working the Land

The ancient Egyptians depended on the yearly cycle of flooding, sowing and harvesting. Low floods and insufficient soil for the crops meant famine. During the growing season, a network of canals and ditches carried water to the fields. Farmers cultivated barley, emmer wheat, vegetables and fruit. Flax was another important crop. Birds and insects often invaded the fields and sometimes violent wind storms flattened the ripening grain. Reapers, who were always men, harvested beneath the hot sun. They listened to flute music and prayed to Isis as they worked. Women never handled tools with blades. They winnowed grain, tossing it into the air so that the wind blew away the light stalks and the heavier seeds fell to the ground. Women also helped to make wine and beer, and pressed oil from nuts and plants. Besides crops, farmers raised cattle, sheep, goats, ducks and geese for food. Tax assessors came every year to gauge the amount of produce that was owed to the government.

THE FARMING ROUND
Farmers worked by the rise and fall of the Nile in a yearly cycle. They never needed fertilisers because the flood soil was so rich.

HARVESTING
At harvest time, every healthy villager worked in the fields. Men cut the crop with sickles. Women and children bound the stalks into sheaves and separated the grain from the chaff.

WHAT DOES THE GARDEN GROW?
The trees with the small fruit are date palms. The ancient Egyptians used dates to sweeten food.

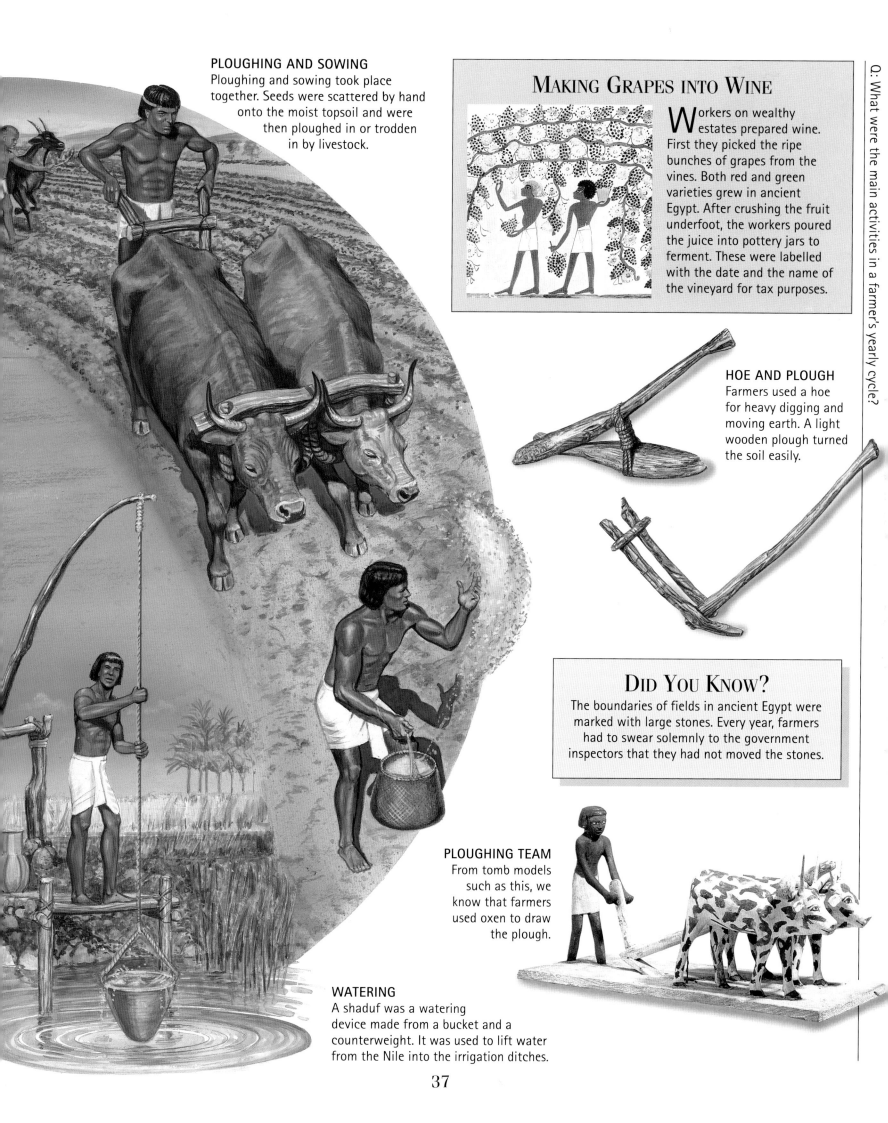

PLOUGHING AND SOWING

Ploughing and sowing took place together. Seeds were scattered by hand onto the moist topsoil and were then ploughed in or trodden in by livestock.

MAKING GRAPES INTO WINE

Workers on wealthy estates prepared wine. First they picked the ripe bunches of grapes from the vines. Both red and green varieties grew in ancient Egypt. After crushing the fruit underfoot, the workers poured the juice into pottery jars to ferment. These were labelled with the date and the name of the vineyard for tax purposes.

HOE AND PLOUGH

Farmers used a hoe for heavy digging and moving earth. A light wooden plough turned the soil easily.

DID YOU KNOW?

The boundaries of fields in ancient Egypt were marked with large stones. Every year, farmers had to swear solemnly to the government inspectors that they had not moved the stones.

PLOUGHING TEAM

From tomb models such as this, we know that farmers used oxen to draw the plough.

WATERING

A shaduf was a watering device made from a bucket and a counterweight. It was used to lift water from the Nile into the irrigation ditches.

37

IN SERVICE
Servants worked on wealthy estates. They did housework and tended the gardens, crops and livestock.

FAMILY CELEBRATION
This tomb painting is like a family photograph. It shows Inhirkha with his wife, son and grandchildren.

AT HOME
The home was a place for the family to relax in. Bigger houses had spacious living quarters with painted walls and high windows, without glass, to help keep the air cool. All homes had places for statues of the household gods.

• LIVING IN THE PAST •

Family Life

Most people in ancient Egypt lived in villages of sunbaked brick houses crammed close together. These had square rooms with small windows, and flat roofs that were often used for cooking. The rich, who were able to employ servants, lived in grander homes with gardens. Twice a day, women fetched water and filled the huge clay vessels that stood in the courtyard or by the doorway of every house. People had very little furniture, especially in the poorer homes. Stools, beds and small tables were the most common pieces; chairs were a sign of importance. Ancient Egyptians usually married within their own social group. Girls became brides when they were about 12; boys married at about fourteen.

TIME FOR BED
Beds were made from wood and woven reeds, and had wooden head-rests for pillows. People did not use bed linen.

STRANGE BUT TRUE
Animals were part of the household. When a pet cat died, the whole family shaved off their eyebrows as a sign of mourning.

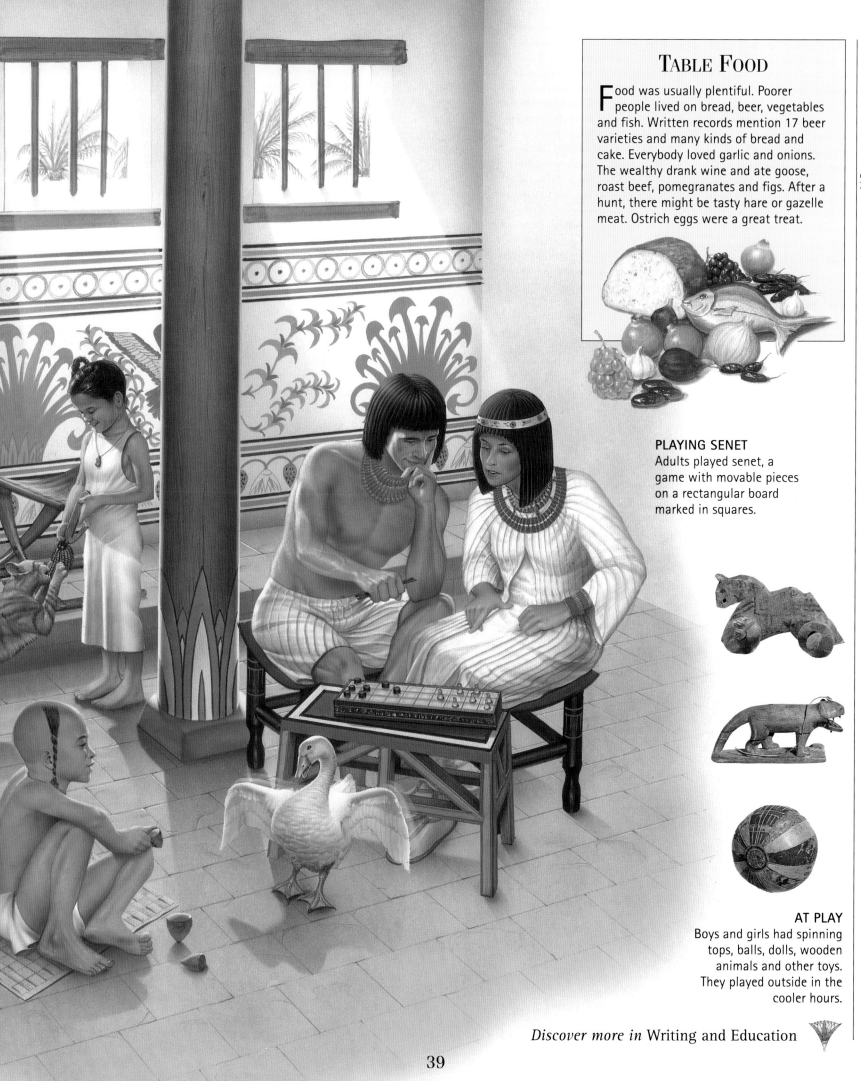

TABLE FOOD

Food was usually plentiful. Poorer people lived on bread, beer, vegetables and fish. Written records mention 17 beer varieties and many kinds of bread and cake. Everybody loved garlic and onions. The wealthy drank wine and ate goose, roast beef, pomegranates and figs. After a hunt, there might be tasty hare or gazelle meat. Ostrich eggs were a great treat.

PLAYING SENET
Adults played senet, a game with movable pieces on a rectangular board marked in squares.

AT PLAY
Boys and girls had spinning tops, balls, dolls, wooden animals and other toys. They played outside in the cooler hours.

Discover more in Writing and Education

39

Dressing Up

ROYAL SANDALS
The upper soles of Tutankhamun's sandals showed Egypt's enemies. He crushed them as he walked.

People in ancient Egypt dressed in light linen clothing made from flax. Weavers used young plants to produce fine, almost see-through fabric for the wealthy, but most people wore garments of coarser texture. The cloth was nearly always white. Pleats, held in place with stiffening starch, were the main form of decoration, but sometimes a pattern of loose threads was woven into the cloth. Slaves or servants, who came from foreign lands, had dresses of patterned fabric. Men dressed in loincloths, kilts and tunic-style shirts. Women had simple, ankle-length sheath dresses with a shawl or cloak for cooler weather. Children usually wore nothing at all. Men and women, rich and poor, owned jewellery and used make-up, especially eye paint. Everybody loved perfume and rubbed scented oils into their skin to protect it against the harsh desert winds.

EYE COLOUR
Favourite eye shadows were green powdered malachite and black crushed lead ore.

REFLECTIONS
Polished bronze or copper mirrors were valued possessions. Their roundness and brightness suggested the sun's life-giving power. Poorer people checked their reflections in water.

THE MEANING OF SPOTS
Some priests wore leopard skins over their shoulders to show their importance. Here, Princess–priestess Nefertiabt is wearing a black-spotted panther skin.

STRANGE BUT TRUE

The ancient Egyptians shaved all their body hair. However, some encouraged the hair on their heads to grow by rubbing their scalps with ointments made from the fat of snakes, crocodiles and hippopotamuses.

STYLISH JEWELLERY

This girdle encircled a woman's waist. The cowrie shells and hair locks were suppose to guarantee health and many children.

COSMETIC CONTAINERS

Face creams, eye paints and body oils were kept in decorative glass, faience and pottery bottles and jars.

BEAUTY AND FASHION

Ancient Egyptians cared greatly about their appearance. The wealthy had servants to launder their clothing and style their wigs.

HAIR AND HAIRDRESSING

Men and women paid great attention to their hair. Some coloured their long tresses with henna. Others shaved their heads or cut their hair short. Wealthier Egyptians owned elaborate wigs made from human hair, which they wore for banquets and ceremonial occasions. Wigs also protected the wearers from sunstroke. In later times, even village women wore wigs when they worked outside.

Discover more in Serving the Gods

Writing and Education

Ancient Egyptians used picture writing, called hieroglyphs, for inscriptions in the tombs and temples. Scribes would tell their sons that to be a scribe "is greater than any other profession". Student scribes took up to ten years to memorise the several hundred hieroglyph signs. They also had lessons in astronomy, mathematics, astrology, practical arts and games and sports. Classroom discipline was strict and teachers believed that "the ears of a boy are on the back. He listens only when he is beaten". The boys who did not become scribes followed in their fathers' footsteps, becoming perhaps farmers or carpenters. Girls stayed at home and learnt music, dancing and housekeeping skills from their mothers.

TAKING NOTE
Students learnt hieratic script first. This running writing was much quicker to do than hieroglyphs.

PRACTICE MAKES PERFECT
Students practised writing on broken bits of stone called ostraca.

HIERATIC SCRIPT
Scribes learnt hieratic writing for listing taxes and recording accounts, and hieroglyphs for writing on tomb walls and monuments.

DID YOU KNOW?

Egypt officially converted to Christianity when the Roman Empire took over in AD 324. Egyptian writing was banned because the Romans considered it to be pagan. People forgot how to write hieroglyphs and nobody learnt how to read them. As a result, hieroglyphs became a lost language.

EVERLASTING WRITING

Carved in hard granite, this cross-legged scribe will write forever on the papyrus spread between his knees.

PAPER FROM REEDS

Paper was made from thinly sliced papyrus stems. One layer was placed on another and the plant's juices glued them together.

SCRIBE SCHOOL

The boys learnt to read and write in groups by copying and reciting texts with wise messages that taught them how to behave properly.

READING THE STONE

Inscriptions on the Rosetta Stone were the key to reading the pyramid texts and other ancient Egyptian writing. The top band is in hieroglyphs. The middle band is in demotic script, a later form of hieratic writing. The bottom band is in Greek. The stone was discovered in 1799. By 1822, Jean-François Champollion, a French scholar, had deciphered some of the letters.

WRITING KIT

A scribe's tools consisted of a palette of coloured paints and brushes made from reeds.

Owl

Water

Bread

Man

Arm

Reed

Mouth

Flax

Basket

Discover more in Social Order

43

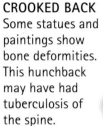
TAWERET
Taweret protected pregnant women. She was depicted as part hippopotamus and part woman, with the legs of a lion.

CROOKED BACK
Some statues and paintings show bone deformities. This hunchback may have had tuberculosis of the spine.

SWEET DREAMS
This hippopotamus ivory wand was used to protect a sleeper from attacks by poisonous night creatures.

EYE OF HORUS
As the two gods struggled for power, Seth tore out Horus's eye. It was magically restored and became a symbol of protective watchfulness.

• LIVING IN THE PAST •

Healing and Magic

Doctors in ancient Egypt set broken bones with wooden splints bound with plant fibres, dressed wounds with oil and honey, and performed surgery with knives, forceps and metal or wooden probes. They had cures for many diseases, some of which they thought were caused by worms such as the "hefet" worm in the stomach or the "fenet" worm that gnawed teeth. Physicians knew that the heart "spoke" through the pulse, but they also thought it controlled everything that happened in the body, and all thoughts and feelings. They did not realise that the brain was important. Plant remedies were popular. Garlic was prescribed for snakebite, to gargle for sore throats and to soothe bruises. Doctors used a vulture's quill to apply eyedrops containing celery juice. When practical medicine failed, physicians turned to magic. People wore amulets to ward off accident and sickness. They also thought some of the gods had healing powers.

A CRIPPLING DISEASE
Priest Remi's shorter, thinner leg was probably the result of poliomyelitis. He would have had this illness as a child.

GOOD LUCK CHARMS

People in ancient Egypt believed that amulets protected them from harm. They wore them as personal jewellery and were buried with them for use in the afterlife. The fish amulet on the girl's plait guarded her against watery accidents such as drowning or being taken by crocodiles. The Bes amulet round her neck saved her from household dangers.

MOTHER AND CHILD
This wooden amulet shows a mother with her baby. It was supposed to ensure a safe childbirth.

WHAT MUMMIES CAN TELL US

Seqenenre II's preserved head shows the severe wounds from which he died. Through autopsies and X-ray examinations of mummies, experts have found out much about the health problems of the ancient Egyptians. They suffered from many of the sicknesses we do, but had no immunisation against infectious diseases such as smallpox and poliomyelitis. Some mummies have badly decayed teeth. Grit and sand in their bread may have worn away their teeth's outer surface, or perhaps ancient Egyptians ate too many cakes sweetened with honey and dates.

Making Things

Many of the objects that tell us how people lived in ancient Egypt were made by potters, stonemasons, carpenters, glassmakers, leatherworkers, metalworkers and jewellers. Most of the cloth made by spinners and weavers has perished, but we know much about their work from friezes in the tombs. The pharaohs kept whole villages of highly skilled craftspeople employed on building projects. Stone for temples, pyramids and statues was collected from the surrounding desert, and copper and gold were plentiful. Some materials had to be imported, particularly timber, ivory, and semi-precious stones such as lapis lazuli and turquoise. As the ancient Egyptians did not use money, workers received their wages in clothes, lodging, bread, onions and beer. Craftspeople worked in communal workshops. Everything they did was part of a team effort and they did not receive special praise for their individual skills.

ISSUING MATERIALS
Metals were weighed before work began. The scales had pans on each end of a horizontal beam resting on a vertical support.

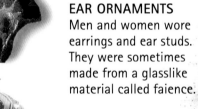

EAR ORNAMENTS
Men and women wore earrings and ear studs. They were sometimes made from a glasslike material called faience.

Axe

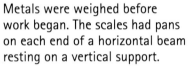
Saw

WORKING WITH WOOD
Woodworkers built or carved furniture. Some of their tools, such as saws and chisels, have not changed much through the years.

PRODUCTION LINE
This crowded workshop shows goldsmiths, carpenters, jewellers and engravers at work.

Adze

FIRE HAZARDS
Working with the hot fire day after day damaged the smelters' lungs and eyes. They were often burnt by flying cinders.

STRANGE BUT TRUE
The first recorded strike in history took place near Thebes where builders had waited two months for their wages. They refused to work and chanted "we are hungry" until they were paid.

FAIENCE BOWL
This bowl is patterned with fish swimming between lotus buds. The lotus, which opens at sunrise and closes at sunset, symbolises rebirth.

BURNING BRIGHT
Smelters had to heat the metal ore in a container to burn off the impurities before they could use the molten metal. They made the fire burn fiercely by blowing on it through hollow reeds tipped with clay nozzles.

WOMEN AT WORK
Women did most of the weaving in ancient Egypt. This wooden model from chancellor Meketre's tomb shows the activity in the textile workshop on his estate. Some workers are walking about spinning linen thread from flax fibres. This will be woven into cloth. The weavers squatting down are operating the two horizontal looms on the floor.

BURIED TREASURE
This solid gold vase was found near the temple of ancient Bubastis. It is hammered in a corn-cob pattern.

BLOWN GLASS
Glassmakers did not learn the blowing technique until the Roman period. Before that, molten glass was moulded around a core.

Discover more in The God-kings

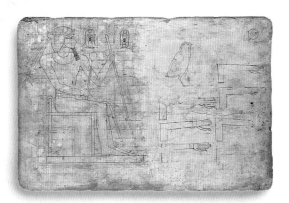

PERFECTING THE ART
This board shows a practice drawing of Tuthmosis III within a grid. The artist seemed to have trouble with the arm hieroglyph.

HEADS RIGHT, EYES FRONT
Artists drew people's eyes and shoulders as if they were seeing them from the front. All other parts of the body were drawn side on. The left leg was always shown in front of the right.

PAINTING SEQUENCE
First, a stonemason smoothed the wall and covered it with a layer of thin plaster. This surface was marked with a square grid made by string dipped in red paint.

PAPYRUS PAINTING
The spells and texts for a person's *Book of the Dead* were painted in bright colours on sheets of papyrus.

• LIVING IN THE PAST •

Artists at Work

Ancient Egyptian paintings told stories about people's lives and what they expected to happen to them after they died and met their gods. Artists painted detailed scenes on houses, temple pillars and the vast walls of tombs, where well-organised teams worked by lamplight in difficult and stuffy conditions. They followed carefully prepared plans of what to paint, and strict rules about the way to show figures and objects. The outline scribes always drew important people larger than anyone else who appeared in the picture. Painters used pigments made from crushed rocks and minerals—green from powdered malachite, red from iron oxide—which they mixed with egg white and gum arabic. The colours in many of the tombs and temples are still as fresh and brilliant as when they were first brushed on the walls more than 5,000 years ago.

GRACEFUL WOMAN
Paint was applied to the plaster-coated cloth that covered the wood on this coffin lid.

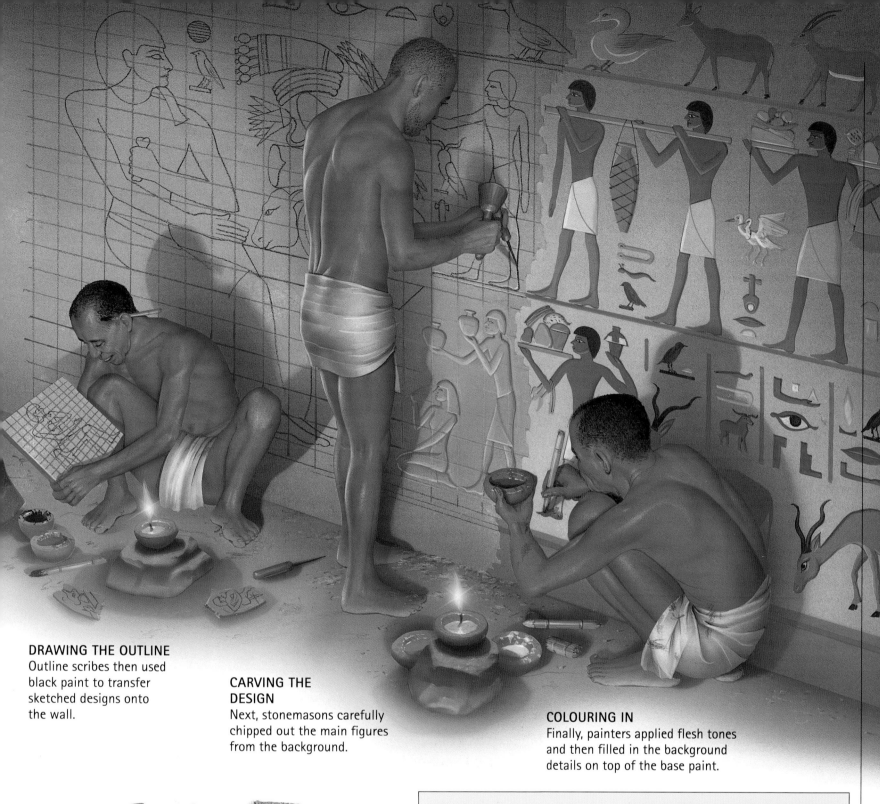

DRAWING THE OUTLINE
Outline scribes then used black paint to transfer sketched designs onto the wall.

CARVING THE DESIGN
Next, stonemasons carefully chipped out the main figures from the background.

COLOURING IN
Finally, painters applied flesh tones and then filled in the background details on top of the base paint.

PAINTING EQUIPMENT
Artists' tools included palettes for diluting paint and wooden brushes with split ends for painting.

AKHENATEN'S STYLE

Pharaoh Akhenaten introduced some changes to the style of art during his 17-year rule. In his city at Amarna, dedicated to the sun-god he called Aten, the artists and sculptors used a more lifelike way of portraying people. This scene, carved in relief, shows Akhenaten giving an earring to his daughter. Queen Nefertiti holds two younger daughters.

KEEPING THE BEAT

These broken pieces of clappers, made of ivory, were once part of percussion instruments musicians used to beat out dance rhythms.

GRACEFUL GYMNASTICS

Dancers performed somersaults, back bends and high-kicks. Weighted discs on the ends of their pigtails swung with the rhythmic movement.

Feasts and Festivals

One hieroglyphic inscription says "be joyful and make merry". Wealthy people loved to invite friends to their homes to share great feasts. The food was plentiful and the wine flowed freely. The hosts hired storytellers, dancers and other entertainers. Ancient Egyptian musicians played many instruments including flutes, clarinets, oboes, lutes, harps, tambourines, cymbals and drums. Poorer people enjoyed themselves on holidays for royal occasions such as the crowning of a pharaoh, and at yearly harvest and religious festivals. Huge crowds gathered for a "coming forth" when the statue of a god was carried in procession outside the temple. Music and acrobatic displays were part of these parades. People made bouquets, garlands and collars from fresh flowers for private banquets and public festivals.

TABLE MANNERS

Banquet guests sat around low tables. They ate with their fingers and afterwards servants brought water to wash their hands.

PERFUMED AIR

Scented cones on the hair melted slowly during a banquet. The perfumed grease released a pleasant fragrance as it ran down over wigs and clothes.

WELCOME GUESTS
Servants handed out scented hair cones at the door. Children often joined in with the festivities.

FESTIVAL OF OPET

The Opet Festival, a yearly holiday, took place during the Nile flood. By the time Ramesses III reigned in 1194 BC, it lasted for 27 days. The statue of the great sun-god Amun-Re, attended by the pharaoh and priests, was carried in procession from Karnak temple south to Luxor temple as shown above. After special ceremonies, the statue was returned to Karnak.

DID YOU KNOW?

Men and women never danced together in ancient Egypt. Dance routines included graceful acrobatics and gymnastics.

THE CAT GODDESS
Bastet, the cat goddess, was the daughter of Re. Her yearly festival was celebrated throughout the land.

AMUSING THE GUESTS
Storytelling and poetry recitals often began the feast. The entertainment became noisier and more energetic as the feasting progressed.

Discover more in Serving the Gods

51

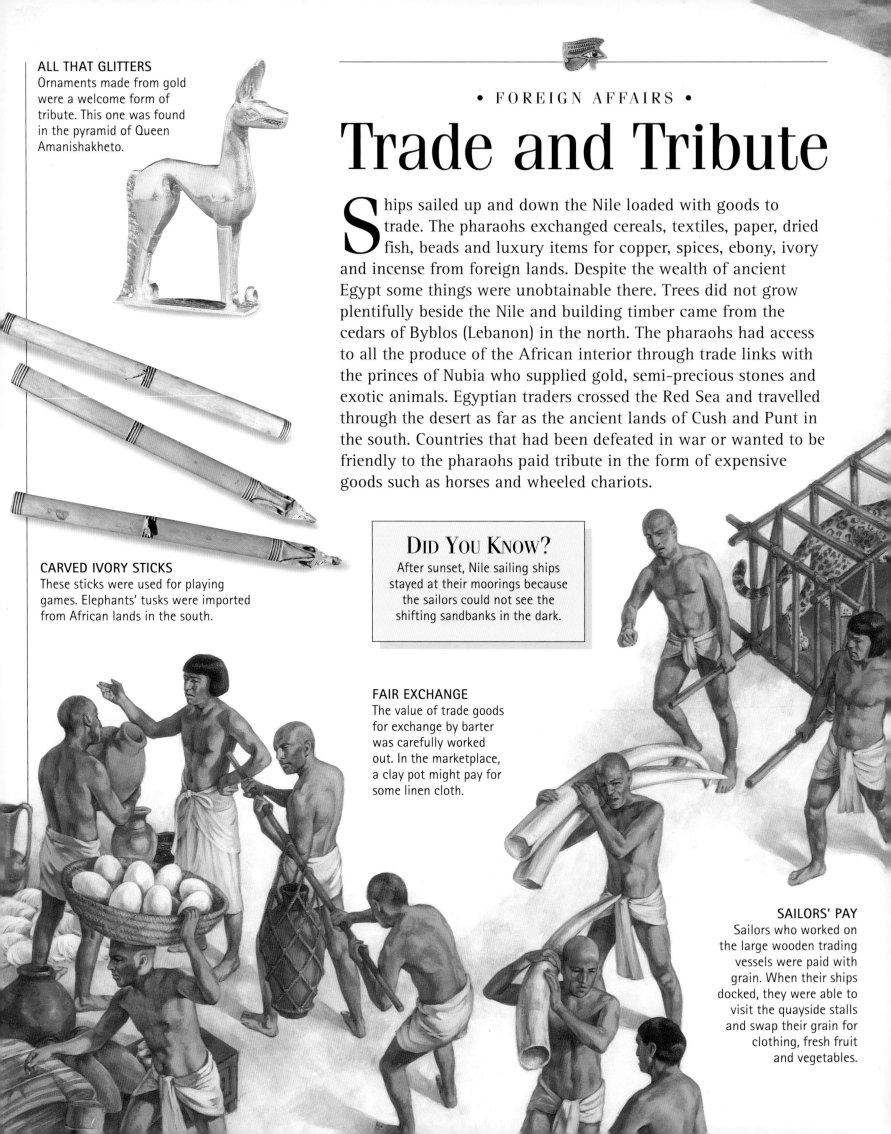

ALL THAT GLITTERS
Ornaments made from gold were a welcome form of tribute. This one was found in the pyramid of Queen Amanishakheto.

Trade and Tribute

Ships sailed up and down the Nile loaded with goods to trade. The pharaohs exchanged cereals, textiles, paper, dried fish, beads and luxury items for copper, spices, ebony, ivory and incense from foreign lands. Despite the wealth of ancient Egypt some things were unobtainable there. Trees did not grow plentifully beside the Nile and building timber came from the cedars of Byblos (Lebanon) in the north. The pharaohs had access to all the produce of the African interior through trade links with the princes of Nubia who supplied gold, semi-precious stones and exotic animals. Egyptian traders crossed the Red Sea and travelled through the desert as far as the ancient lands of Cush and Punt in the south. Countries that had been defeated in war or wanted to be friendly to the pharaohs paid tribute in the form of expensive goods such as horses and wheeled chariots.

CARVED IVORY STICKS
These sticks were used for playing games. Elephants' tusks were imported from African lands in the south.

DID YOU KNOW?
After sunset, Nile sailing ships stayed at their moorings because the sailors could not see the shifting sandbanks in the dark.

FAIR EXCHANGE
The value of trade goods for exchange by barter was carefully worked out. In the marketplace, a clay pot might pay for some linen cloth.

SAILORS' PAY
Sailors who worked on the large wooden trading vessels were paid with grain. When their ships docked, they were able to visit the quayside stalls and swap their grain for clothing, fresh fruit and vegetables.

COUNTING THE CARGO
All foreign trade goods belonged to the pharaoh. Scribes kept careful records of the cargoes as they were unloaded.

FOUR-FOOTED SUBJECTS
Some pharaohs liked having wild animals from other countries to decorate their courts. We do not know how many of these creatures failed to survive the journeys.

TRIBUTE FROM THE SOUTHLANDS
Gifts to Pharaoh Sebekhotepe included gold rings, giraffes' tails, ebony logs, jasper, a leopard skin and live baboons on leashes.

SEA VOYAGES

The methods of travel in ancient times meant that trading expeditions could take several years. The ancient Egyptians carried their boats in pieces across the desert and assembled them on the shores of the Red Sea. This scene from Queen Hatshepsut's temple shows incense trees being loaded onto ships visiting the land of Punt. The roots were placed in baskets for the long voyage back to Egypt and then were planted in the temple gardens.

GOLDEN BRACELETS
Queen Ahhotep's bracelets were set with imported semi-precious stones—turquoise, carnelian and lapis lazuli.

Discover more in Working the Land

Defending the Kingdom

CLOSE COMBAT
Daggers and short swords were deadly weapons for hand-to-hand fighting at close quarters. The blades were riveted to the handles.

For centuries, ancient Egyptians needed no permanent army. Egyptians seldom had to defend themselves against enemies, other than Libyan tribes who attacked occasionally from the Western Desert. After the Middle Kingdom, however, the Hyksos from the Near East seized Lower Egypt. They had curved swords, strong bows, body armour and horse-drawn chariots. The Egyptians copied these weapons and began training efficient soldiers. Their new army drove out the hated Hyksos and pushed them back through Palestine and Syria. Prisoners of war were forced to join the army or work as slaves. Egyptians built mudbrick forts, with massive towers surrounded by ditches, to defend their borders. Later, Ramesses III formed a navy of wooden galleys powered by oars and sails, and trapped the slower sailing ships of pirates invading from the Mediterranean Sea.

TUTANKHAMUN'S CHARIOT
This scene pictures a victorious Tutankhamun alone in his chariot. In real life he would have had a driver with him.

PRISONERS OF WAR
Enemies of the pharaoh were always shown with their hands bound or handcuffed.

DID YOU KNOW?
Lions represented courage in ancient Egypt. One poem said that Ramesses II fought "like a fierce lion in a valley of goats".

THE RULES OF WAR
A king in the ancient world led his army to fight the enemy on an open battlefield. The army waited for a signal to begin. There were few surprise attacks and no battles after dark.

CEREMONIAL AXE
This ceremonial axe belonged to the pharaoh Ahmose. The blade shows scenes celebrating his success in driving the Hyksos out of Egypt.

OFF TO WAR

These wooden soldiers, marching in step and carrying shields and lances, represent a troop from one of the nomes of ancient Egypt. Foot soldiers trained for the army from boyhood. They had to live in barracks where discipline was very tough. Upper-class youths usually joined the chariot corps, which was organised quite separately. Successful battle commanders received "Gold of Bravery" flies, like the ones above, as rewards for attacking the enemy again and again.

BATTLE TACTICS

Archers fired from moving chariots. They advanced on the enemy's foot soldiers and then doubled back and attacked from behind.

Discover more in Making Things

MIXED RELIGION
Although Greek pharaohs worshipped their own gods, relief carvings on the temple of Edfu show Ptolemy III and Ptolemy XII with Egyptian deities.

DRINKING CUPS
This Nubian pottery was made on a wheel and decorated with painted and stamped designs.

CHANGING GOVERNMENT
After the Nubian invasion, ancient Egypt was overrun repeatedly by foreigners. For more than a thousand years, power in the ancient world shifted from one conqueror to another.

• FOREIGN AFFAIRS •

Collapse of an Empire

Many of the pharaohs who came after Ramesses III were not strong rulers. Their subjects began to disobey the laws and robbers plundered the tombs. Meanwhile, other countries in the ancient world were growing stronger. Foreign conquerors overran the Egyptian empire and invaded the country itself—first the Nubians, then the Assyrians and later the Persians. Alexander the Great brought his army to help the Egyptians expel the Persians. Ptolemy, one of Alexander's generals, founded a dynasty whose rulers spoke Greek and worshipped Greek gods. The Romans took over from the Greeks. Christianity spread through the Roman Empire and came to ancient Egypt. When the Arabs invaded in the seventh century AD, Fustat became their first capital, Islam became the state religion and Arabic became the official language.

PERSIANS IN POWER
The Persians introduced camels into ancient Egypt. These could move across the desert from one oasis to another.

GOLD COIN
The Greeks brought coins into Egypt. Pharaoh Ptolemy I is portrayed on this gold piece.

ASSYRIANS IN POWER
The well-organised Assyrian army, equipped with iron weapons, swept through ancient Egypt. The Assyrians appointed Egyptian governors to run the country.

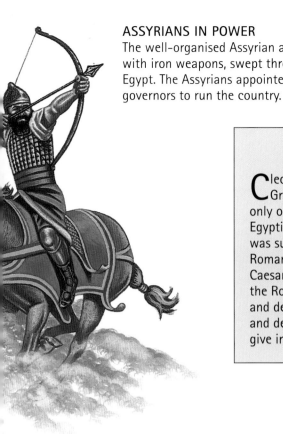

CLEOPATRA

Cleopatra VII was the last Greek pharaoh and the only one who learned the Egyptian language. She was supported by two Roman generals, Julius Caesar and Mark Antony. When Augustus gained power over the Roman Empire, he declared war on Antony and Cleopatra and defeated them in 31 BC. Augustus arrived in Alexandria and demanded Cleopatra's surrender. She was too proud to give in and committed suicide.

ROMANS IN POWER
Emperor Augustus gained power in 30 BC. The Romans sent gold from the desert mines back to Rome.

GREEKS IN POWER
In 332 BC, Alexander the Great took possession of ancient Egypt. Later, the Egyptian city of Alexandria became the leading city in the Greek world.

ROMAN PORTRAIT
Portraits on coffins became more lifelike during the Roman period. Artists mixed paint with melted beeswax to brighten the colours.

DID YOU KNOW?
Early Christian hermits made their homes in some of the royal tombs at Thebes. They lived in the chapels or offering rooms, not in the actual burial chambers.

SOLDIERS' FOOTWEAR
Archaeologists have found Roman shoes, coins and military equipment at an army outpost in Nubia.

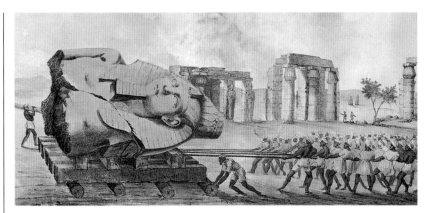

• FOREIGN AFFAIRS •

Discovering Ancient Egypt

How can you discover ancient Egypt? You can visit the pharaohs' treasures in the world's great museums. You can read travellers' tales recorded by writers of the past, such as the Greek historian Herodotus, and you can learn from Egyptologists. When Napoleon Bonaparte's army invaded Egypt in 1798, the French discovered many of its ancient treasures. Since then, Egyptologists have studied monuments, painted friezes, objects from the tombs and things people threw away that the dry climate has preserved. They have deciphered records of daily events and other writing that survives on stone and papyrus. If you ever visit Egypt, you will be able to see the people who now live beside the Nile. They still use some of the old farming methods and tools have changed little since ancient times. But their crops no longer depend on the time of inundation or flooding because the Aswan Dam now controls Egypt's lifeline.

SAVING THE SPHINX
The great Sphinx at Giza is showing its age. From time to time expert restorers have erected scaffolding to make repairs.

58

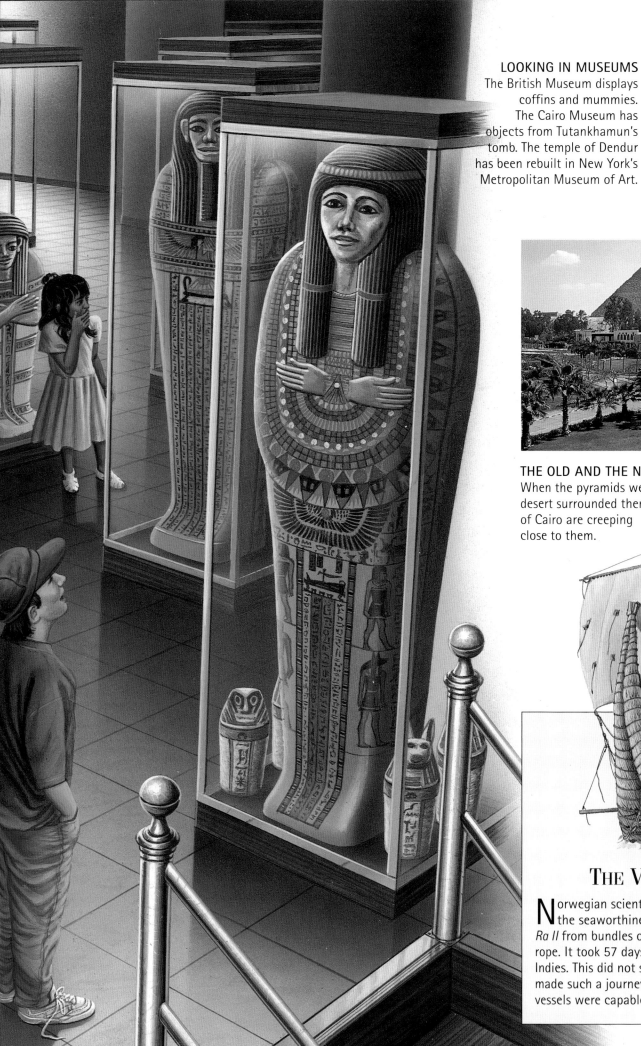

LOOKING IN MUSEUMS

The British Museum displays coffins and mummies. The Cairo Museum has objects from Tutankhamun's tomb. The temple of Dendur has been rebuilt in New York's Metropolitan Museum of Art.

DID YOU KNOW?

To save them from the rising waters of Lake Nasser, the temples from Philae Island were taken piece by piece to Agilkia Island and rebuilt.

THE OLD AND THE NEW

When the pyramids were built at Giza, desert surrounded them. Now, the suburbs of Cairo are creeping close to them.

THE VOYAGE OF *RA II*

Norwegian scientist Thor Heyerdahl wanted to test the seaworthiness of reed boats. In 1970, he built *Ra II* from bundles of papyrus lashed together with rope. It took 57 days to sail from Morocco to the West Indies. This did not show that the ancient Egyptians made such a journey, but it did prove that papyrus vessels were capable of surviving long sea voyages.

Discover more in Set in Stone

Dynasties of Ancient Egypt

Egyptologists have pieced together the sequence of the kings of ancient Egypt from fragments of inscribed stone and papyrus. Generally, a dynasty lasted for the time one family or group of pharaohs was in power. There were three very successful periods. During the Old Kingdom, the first pyramid at Saqqara and the Great Pyramid at Giza were built. In the Middle Kingdom, trade expanded and arts, crafts and temple building flourished. The Hyksos were expelled at the beginning of the New Kingdom and the pharaohs of this time established an empire. Listed here are some of the important kings of ancient Egypt and the approximate dates of their reigns.

2920–2575 BC	**ARCHAIC PERIOD**
2920–2770	**1st Dynasty**
2770–2649	**2nd Dynasty**
2649–2575	**3rd Dynasty**
	2630–2611 Djoser
	2611–2603 Sekhemkhet

Polished clay bowl

2575–2134 BC	**OLD KINGDOM**
2575–2465	**4th Dynasty**
	2551–2528 Khufu
	2520–2494 Khephren
	2490–2472 Menkaure
2465–2323	**5th Dynasty**
2323–2150	**6th Dynasty**
	2289–2255 Pepy I
	2246–2152 Pepy II
2150–2134	**7th-8th Dynasties**

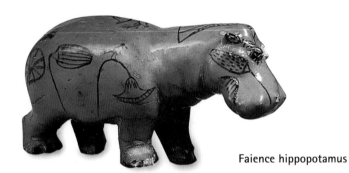

Golden head of a falcon

2134–2040 BC	**1ST INTERMEDIATE PERIOD**
	9th–10th Dynasties
	11th (Theban) Dynasty

Golden serpent

2040–1640 BC	**MIDDLE KINGDOM**
2040–1991	**11th Dynasty (all Egypt)**
	2061–2010 Mentuhotpe

Faience hippopotamus

1991–1783	**12th Dynasty**
	1991–1962 Amenemhet I
	1971–1926 Senwosret I
	1929–1892 Amenemhet II
	1897–1878 Senwosret II
	1878–1841 Senwosret III
	1844–1797 Amenemhet III
	1799–1787 Amenemhet IV
	1787–1783 Nefrusobk
1783–1640	**13th-14th Dynasties**

Tomb stela of Amenemhet I

1640–1550 BC **2ND INTERMEDIATE PERIOD**

15th (Hyksos) Dynasty

16th–17th Dynasties

1550–1070 BC **NEW KINGDOM**

1550–1307 **18th Dynasty**
1550–1525	Ahmose
1525–1504	Amenophis I
1504–1492	Tuthmosis I
1492–1479	Tuthmosis II
1479–1425	Tuthmosis III
1473–1458	Hatshepsut
1427–1401	Amenophis II
1401–1391	Tuthmosis IV
1391–1353	Amenophis III
1353–1335	Amenophis IV/Akhenaten
1335–1333	Smenkhkare
1333–1323	Tutankhamun
1323–1319	Aya
1319–1307	Haremhab

1307–1196 **19th Dynasty**
1307–1306	Ramesses I
1306–1290	Sethos I
1290–1224	Ramesses II
1224–1214	Merneptah
1214–1204	Sethos II
1204–1198	Siptah
1198–1196	Twosre

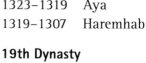

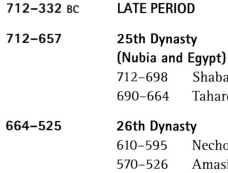

The goddess Selket

1196–1070 **20th Dynasty**
1196–1194	Sethnakhte
1194–1094	Ramesses 111–XI

1070–712 BC **3RD INTERMEDIATE PERIOD**

21st–24th Dynasties

Bust of Akhenaten

712–332 BC **LATE PERIOD**

712–657 **25th Dynasty (Nubia and Egypt)**
712–698	Shabaka
690–664	Taharqa

664–525 **26th Dynasty**
610–595	Necho II
570–526	Amasis

525–404 **27th Dynasty (Persian)**
521–486	Darius I
486–466	Xerxes I

404–399 **28th Dynasty**

399–380 **29th Dynasty**

380–343 **30th Dynasty**
380–362	Nectanebo I

343–332 **31st Dynasty (Persian)**

332 BC–AD 395 **GRECO-ROMAN PERIOD**
332–323	Alexander III the Great
304–284	Ptolemy I
246–221	Ptolemy III
51–30	Cleopatra VII Q
30 BC–AD 14	Augustus

Canopic jars

Glossary

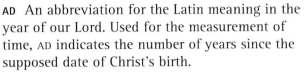

Faience make-up holder

Tomb painting

Cartouches

Ceremonial axe

Wooden porter

AD An abbreviation for the Latin meaning in the year of our Lord. Used for the measurement of time, AD indicates the number of years since the supposed date of Christ's birth.

amulet A charm or piece of jewellery worn as protection against evil.

ankh A symbol that meant life. It was carried by gods and pharaohs. Later, the ankh was adopted as a Christian symbol.

Ba An Egyptian word for a person's spirit, rather like the word soul.

bartering A system of trade by which goods of the same value are exchanged and money is not used.

BC Before Christ. Used for the measurement of time, BC indicates the number of years before the supposed date of Christ's birth.

Black Land The fertile soil in the River Nile valley and delta. The Egyptians called this land *kemet*.

Book of the Dead Sheets of papyrus paper covered with magic texts and pictures. These were placed with the dead to help them pass through the dangers of the underworld.

canopic jars Small jars for storing the organs of a dead person when the body was mummified.

Carnarvon, Lord (1866–1923) The wealthy fifth Earl of Carnarvon from England who contributed the funds for Howard Carter's expeditions to excavate Egyptian tombs. He died in Cairo shortly after the spectacular discovery of Tutankhamun's tomb in 1922.

carnelian A red semi-precious stone from the eastern desert.

Carter, Howard (1874–1939) An English Egyptologist who found the tombs of Hatshepsut, Tuthmosis IV and Tutankhamun.

cartonnage A material made from scraps of linen or papyrus gummed together with plaster or resin. Cartonnage was light and strong and often used for mummy cases instead of wood.

cartouche An oval shape surrounding the pair of hieroglyphs depicting the name of a pharaoh.

Champollion, Jean-François (1790–1832) An expert in oriental languages and French founder of Egyptology who deciphered the hieroglyphic inscription on the Rosetta Stone in 1822.

civilisation An organised society that has developed social customs, government, technology and the arts.

crook A stick with a curved top carried by a god or pharaoh to symbolise kingship.

Cush A country to the south of ancient Egypt, probably where North Sudan is now.

deben A metal ring used by traders for measuring weight. One deben weighed about 90 gm (4 ounces).

demotic script A form of writing that developed from hieratic script from 700 BC onwards. It was used for administration and business.

dolerite A hard rock used by the ancient Egyptians to grind and crush other rocks.

dynasty A ruling family. Thirty-one dynasties ruled ancient Egypt during its long history.

Egyptologist A special kind of archaeologist who finds out about how people lived in ancient Egypt by studying the things they left behind.

embalmer A person who treats a dead body with spices and oils to stop it decaying.

faience A glasslike material used for making cups, jars and amulets. It was made by heating up powdered quartz in a mould.

flail A tool carried by a god or pharaoh to symbolise kingship and the fertility of the land.

flax A plant from which thread can be made and woven into linen.

frieze A strip of painting or carving on a temple or a tomb wall that told a story.

gild To cover in gold leaf.

gold leaf A very thin sheet of beaten gold.

gum arabic A gum from trees used by the ancient Egyptians as a paint fixative.

Herodotus A Greek historian and traveller who lived from about 485 BC to 425 BC. He wrote about his impressions of ancient Egypt.

hieratic script A faster form of writing than hieroglyphs. It was always written from right to left, unlike European languages, which are written from left to right.

hieroglyphs The symbols and pictures of ancient Egyptian writing.

Hyksos people Foreigners, probably from Palestine or Syria, who invaded Egypt.

incense An aromatic substance extracted from resin. Incense was used in ritual ceremonies.

irrigate To channel water from a river or a lake to land through a system of canals and ditches.

Ka An Egyptian word for a person's life force created at birth and released by death.

lapis lazuli A dark blue semi-precious stone from the mines of what is now Afghanistan.

malachite A copper ore. When crushed, it was used as green eye paint and symbolised fertility.

mummification A process of drying and embalming that preserves the dead body of a person or an animal.

natron A natural salt from the desert that absorbs moisture. The ancient Egyptians used it for mummification.

nomarch An official in charge of a province or region called a nome. There were 42 nomes in ancient Egypt.

oasis (singular), **oases** (plural) A fertile patch in the desert with its own water supply.

ostracon (singular), **ostraca** (plural) A fragment of pottery or large flake of stone used by students to practise their writing.

palette A flat piece of wood or stone on which artists mixed paints.

papyrus A reed that the ancient Egyptians made into paper and other objects.

pharaoh The ruler of ancient Egypt. The name comes from the ancient Egyptian word *per-ao*, meaning the great house. It referred to the palace where the pharaoh lived.

pigment A powder that is mixed with a liquid to make ink or paint.

Punt A country to the southeast of ancient Egypt, probably in the region of modern Eritrea.

Red Land The desert that lay beyond the river valley and delta. The ancient Egyptians called this land *deshret*.

relief A shallow carving on a stone surface.

ritual The procedure for a religious ceremony such as the Opening of the Mouth.

Rosetta Stone An inscribed slab of granite that gave the major clue to deciphering hieroglyphs. It was found by a French soldier near the village of Rosetta in 1799. The stone is 114 cm (3 ft 7 in) high, 72 cm (2 ft 3 in) wide, 28 cm (11 in) thick and weighs 762 kg (1,684 pounds). The Rosetta Stone is now in London's British Museum.

sarcophagus (singular), **sarcophagi** (plural) A large stone box that enclosed a mummy's coffin. The surfaces were usually carved in relief.

senet A game played by the Egyptians with a board and counters. It had lucky and unlucky squares and was a little like the modern game of draughts.

shabti A model figure that acted as the servant of the deceased and carried out all the work required in the afterlife.

shaduf An irrigation device made from a bucket and a counterweight. It transferred water from the Nile into canals.

silt Mud washed over the river banks during the time of flood.

time of emergence A season of four months from November to February.

time of harvest A season of four months from March to June.

time of inundation The yearly flooding of the Nile valley from July to October.

tributary A stream of water that flows into a larger stream of water. The Egyptian Nile's main tributaries were the Blue Nile and the White Nile.

turquoise A blue-green stone imported from the Sinai Peninsula.

vizier Chief adviser to the pharaoh and second only to him in importance. At times there were two viziers.

Tutankhamun's gold funeral mask

Hair comb and toys

Pyramids at Giza

Rosetta Stone

Crocodile mummy

Index

Picture Credits

(t=top, b=bottom, l=left, r=right, c=centre, i=icon, F=front, C=cover, B=back, Bg=background)
Ashmolean Museum, Oxford, 44ct. Austral International, 33tr (Colorific!/Terence Spencer). Australian Picture Library, 32tc (D.&J. Heaton), 51tr. Bildarchiv Pressischer Kulturbesitz, 9br (Vatican Museum, Rome), 18tl, 21br, 63tr (Egyptian Museum, Cairo), 35br (Egyptian Museum, Cairo/M. Büsing), 61tc (Egyptian Museum, Cairo/J. Liepe), 10bc (Staatliche Museen, Berlin). British Museum, 6cl, 7br, 7tl, 14cl, 14tr, 15br, 15tc, 15tr, 16tr, 17cr, 19cr, 20tl, 20tr, 21tr, 22/23b, 22c, 23cl, 23cr, 23t, 35cr, 37br, 37tr, 39cr, 41br, 41tr, 42tr, 43bc, 44c, 46bc, 46cl, 46bl, 47br, 48cr, 48tl, 50br, 52tl, 53cr, 56tc, 57br, 57tr, 58tl, 61r, 62tl, 63bcr, 63tcr. Continuum Productions Corporation, 16bc (R. Wood). C. M. Dixon, 56bc. Enrico Ferorelli, 21tl. Griffith Institute, Ashmolean Museum, 18tc, 19tr, 28cl, 29tl. Hirmer Fotoarchiv, Munich, 50tc. The Image Bank, 26cl, 63cr (R. Lockyer). John Rylands University Library of Manchester, 32tr. Jürgen Liepe, 8bl, 8br, 8bc, 11br, 12bl,

13tc, 14cbl, 22cr, 23c, 25br, 25tl, 27bl, 28br, 29tr 38tl, 47cr, 47tr, 48bc, 48cl, 49bl, 49br, 50tl, 53br, 54bl, 54br, 55cc, 55tr, 60br, 60bc, 60cr, 60cl, 60tr, 61bc, 62bl, 63br. Manchester Museum, 52cl (Neg. no. 2138). Giulio Mezzetti, 53bl. Musees Royaux D'Art, 44tcl. National Geographic Society, 31bc (V. Boswell), 30tl, 58bc (O.L. Mazzatenta). National Museums of Scotland, 7bcl. Ny Carlsberg Glyptotek, 44bl. Picture Media, 29bl (Francolon-Gaillarde/Gamma). Robert Harding Picture Library, 54cl, 54tl (F.L. Kenett), 56tl (T. Wood), 15bl, 17br, 26tl, 32bl, 59tr. A.J. Spencer, 6tl. St. Thomas' Hospital, 19br (S. W. Hughes). Thames & Hudson Limited, 20bl. Geoff Thompson, 10cl, 62cl. Werner Forman Archive, 7cbr, 14tl, 43tr, 45tr, 50bl (British Museum), 24bc, 43c, 44tr (Egyptian Museum, Cairo), 46c (Petrie Museum, University College, London), 22tr (Royal Musem of Art and History, Brussels), 36bl, 38tc (E. Strouhal), 40bl (The Louvre), 7bc, 30tr, 45br.

Illustration Credits

Paul Bachem, 34/35c, 34tr, 35tr. Kerri Gibbs, 46/47c, 46tl. Mike Gorman, 25cr, 30tc, 31tl. Christa Hook/Bernard Thornton Artists, UK, 52/53c. Richard Hook/Bernard Thornton Artists, UK, 2/3, 10/11c, 10tc, 11tr, 20/21c, 27–30c, 50/51c. Janet Jones, 4bc, 4tr, 5bc, 12/13c, 13tr, 16l, 16c, 16/17c, 17tr, 42/43c, 42tl, 43cr, 43r. Iain McKellar, 1, 4l, 5br, 14/15c, 18/19c, 24/25c, 25bc. Peter Mennim, 40/41c, 45c. Paul Newman, 56/57c, 57tc. Darren Pattenden/Garden Studio, 38/39c, 38bl, 39tr, 48/49c. Evert Ploeg, 26/31c. Trevor Ruth, 32/33c, 58/59c. Ray Sim, 6/7c, 7bl, 7cl, 7tr, 59br. Mark Sofilas, 8/9c, 9bc. C. Winston Taylor, 36/37c, 37cr, 54/55c. Steve Trevaskis, 4br, 5tr, 6br, 27br, 28bc, 40tr. Rod Westblade, endpapers, icons.

Cover Credits

Australian Museum, Bg (C. Bento) Werner Forman Archive, BCtl (Egyptian Museum, Cairo) Jürgen Liepe, BCr, FCtl Peter Mennim, FCb Ray Sim, FCtr